# Blood Unbound:

# A Loki Devotional

*art by Dyri Vixen, dip pen and India ink*

# Blood Unbound:

# A Loki Devotional

edited by Bat Collazo

Troth Publications
2021

Published by The Troth
325 Chestnut Street, Suite 800
Philadelphia, PA 19106
http://www.thetroth.org/

ISBN: 978-1-941136-48-5 (paperback)
978-1-941136-49-2 (hardcover)
978-1-941136-50-8 (PDF)
978-1-941136-51-5 (EPUB)
978-1-941136-52-2 (MOBI)

Cover: Sae Lokason
Troth logo designed by Kveldúlfr Gundarsson; drawn by 13 Labs, Chicago, Illinois
Typeset in Adobe Garamond Pro 10/12

# DEDICATION

*Sonr Laufeyjar*
*Hrafn-Ásar vinr*
*Farmr arma Sigynjar*
*Firna-slægjan Fárbauta mögr*

*Bölvasmiðr*
*Rógberi ásanna*
*Hugreynandi Hœnis*
*Geðreynir Gauts herþrumu*

*Faðir Nara*
*Faðir Ála*
*Faðir Heljar*
*Faðir Vánargands*

*Faðir lögseims*
*Áss ragr*
*Sleipnis frændi*
*Goða dólgr*

*Inn bundni áss*
*Inn slægi áss*
*Rög vættr*
*Hveðrungr*

*Loptr*
*Lóðurr*
*Lævísi Loki*
*Vé*

*Hail Loki,*
*blood in my veins and ants in my pants,*
*swallower of my heart.*
*Be welcome.*

*Loki carried off by Thjazi in eagle form.*
*Illustration by Dorothy Hardy, from Hélène Guerber,* Myths of the Norsemen *(1919)*

# CONTENTS

# EDITOR'S FOREWORD

At Trothmoot 2019, The Return of Loki, during a morning Troth Publications report in the mess hall at Fort Flagler, Luke Babb turned to me and asked under their breath, "Should we do a Loki book?"

"Yes," I said.

Welcome to the Loki book.

I am blessed with the knowledge that "we" means the communities of those who also worship Loki. In the Troth, this community has existed long before my presence here, in the entirety of the organization's history. But we built momentum during the creative energy formed that weekend in late June 2019, where I and others—many of us attending for the first time *because* of Loki—could speak our beloved god's name over the horn, surrounded by others with eyes as wet and bright as our own.

Since that time, I acquired the role of editor-in-chief—a labor of love, but not alone. Loki's family tree is sprawling and tangled, and so I am delighted that this book is not an individual's book, but a community's book. This is only a small snapshot of a wide, diverse group of people, but as it is, I'm delighted that 16 contributors—some of whom I know very well, some of whom were previously strangers to me—were able to share their voices and their devotion to Loki.

For me, heading this project, what does that devotion mean?

In Saxo Grammaticus' *Gesta Danorum* (early 13th century), Thorkil journeys outside the bounds of the known, safer world, to "a country where the unchanging face of darkness repressed any alteration of light".[1] There, he encounters a figure bound in a cave: "Utgard-Loki".

Norse myth, of course, is never simple fact. Like an increasingly disjointed game of telephone, oral histories—passed down through the years, then recorded, then re-recorded—shift and evolve. Though I suspect Utgard-Loki in Snorri Sturluson's *Gylfaginning* is a different figure than the Loki of this devotional, Saxo's Loki of the Outskirts, Loki of the Other World, leans so close to Loki's binding that I choose to interpret this piece as one version of *my* Loki.

---

1. Davidson, Hilda Ellis. *The History of the Danes, Books I-IX.* Fisher, Peter, translator. D.S. Brewer, 2002. p. 269.

"From here the visitors could see a murky, repulsive chamber, inside which they descried Utgartha-Loki, his hands and feet laden with a huge weight of fetters. His rank-smelling hairs were as long and tough as spears of cornel-wood. . . such a powerful stench rolled over the bystanders that they had to smother their nostrils in their cloaks and could scarcely breathe. They had hardly gained the open air when the snakes flew from every direction and spat over them. . . toxic rain."[2]

King Gorm—who previously survived starvation by praying to Utgard-Loki and receiving a fair weather spell in return[3]—anxiously awaits news of his deity from Thorkil, after foreboding dreams. Thorkil describes Utgard-Loki's binding, and the king is devastated.

Though this segment of the story is supplemented by some heavy-handed Christian moralizing on Saxo's part, readers could also find a narrative of devotional passion to the extreme:

"Listening with avid ears to all the other parts of the narrative, when at last his own deity was unfavourably described he could not stand it. He was unable to bear hearing this ugly and invidious report of Utgartha-Loki and was so grief-stricken about the god's vile state that he gave up the ghost at the unendurable words, even while Thorkil was in the middle of his tale. And so, while he continued to cherish dearly the veneration of this futile divinity, he came to learn where the true prison of sorrows lay."[4]

Modern Lokeans—especially when dismissed more recently as "teenage Marvel fangirls" by other Heathens—are often stereotyped as immature, unacceptably feminine, and hyperemotional. In this 800-year-old story, we see an old king so passionate about loving Loki and so upset about his binding that he dies on the spot.

And so I say in response to King Gorm, as both a tongue-in-cheek joke and a reclamation: what a mood.

Lokeans consist of all sorts of ages, experience levels, and genders, with never any singular way of existing, feeling, or doing worship. But some of

2. Ibid. p. 269.
3. Ibid. p. 267.
4. Ibid. p. 270.

us—dare I say most of us—do have an intense emotional connection to Loki. This love permeates each piece in this book, even as the expression of it changes.

How did I and other Lokeans arrive here? Why do we dare? Loki, many say, is not an easy god.

If Ásatrúar are the ones proclaiming this, my snark reaction tends to be: Have you even *met* Odin?

My less concise response, however, is this: easy? What deity truly is? What *beings*, with all our intricacies and contradictions, are easy on the inside? It doesn't seem right to ask any fierce, vibrant force to be reduced to palatability. No, Loki is not easy. But for me, Loki is easy to love, all the more because he is complicated, ambivalent, ambiguous, unexpected.

Hafez, a Persian mystic poet and Sufi Muslim from the 14th century[5]— known for subtle jabs at religious hypocrisy even as he expressed the beauty of the divine—brings Loki to mind for me in the poem "Tired of Speaking Sweetly," which begins: "Love wants to reach out and manhandle us, / Break all our teacup talk of God." He describes the ways the divine Beloved helps break humanity's world for the better, tearing what doesn't serve us from our grasps. Ironically, when faced with this gift, "Most everyone I know / Quickly packs their bags and hightails it / Out of town."[6]

I am reminded of Loki, too, when reading many of Octavia Butler's *Parable of the Sower* (1993) quotes, linked to a spirituality called Earthseed. "God is Change," for instance, and: "A gift of God / May sear unready fingers".[7] No Heathen gods are only one thing, for me. None are easily reduced to "God of XYZ," least of all Loki. But one of many things Loki brings to my life, and the life of many others, is change.

It's no secret that the border-straddling Loki (Æsir and Jotun, friend and enemy of the gods, shapeshifter of many forms and many genders, creator as Lodurr and destroyer as Worldbreaker) sometimes draws the attention of border-straddling devotees. This is true for my experience.

---

5. Darke, Diana. "The book in every Iranian home." *BBC News*, 2 November 2014. https://www.bbc.com/news/magazine-29648166
6. Hafiz (Daniel Landinsky, transl.) *The Gift*. Penguin Compass, 1999. p. 187-188.
7. Butler, Octavia. "The Book of the Living I". *Earthseed*. https://godischange.org/the-book-of-the-living/

I met Loki in this lifetime in the late 1990s. I was a mixed race, repressed baby queer, in a 2e school program for children both gifted and challenged. My classmate and friend—a literal border-crosser as a recent Chinese immigrant, openly bi and genderqueer (before we knew these words), openly Wiccan—worshipped Loki. I was raised Roman Catholic, and coerced for years to stay that way—but I was fascinated by my friend, and fascinated by their god.

Loki and I have been through a lot since then, including the years between this childhood encounter and my adult polytheistic practice. I suspect I was not ever forgotten, even as I forgot him, for a while. On November 1st, 2017, I oathed myself to Loki.

Not everything Loki has brought to my life has been comfortable. Sometimes I've even struggled against it, though I'm getting better at acting on the open, unrestricted trust I offer to Loki, my *fulltrui*. Loki has been integral in helping me unlock the joy that comes from knowing myself in my wholeness, and he never allows me to stagnate.

Loki, border-crosser, line-straddler, occupied an ambiguous position in the Troth's policies from 2009 until January 1, 2019, when the "Loki Ban" was rescinded. This ten-year policy did not restrict individual members from worshipping Loki, but did prevent him from being hailed at Troth-sponsored events, including but not limited to Trothmoots—marginalizing his worship to "unofficial" rituals outside of formal Troth space.

I myself arrived in the Troth at the tail end of this policy, just in time for the online debates to heat up again, just in time to achieve full membership and vote on the ban's removal. But others who love Loki have been here much longer, speaking out. For instance, in the midst of the ban, Lagaria Farmer wrote:

> . . . Himself has always been with me and always will be, making sure I make the necessary decisions and changes, being a holy catalyst in my life, and will offer comfort—or a swift kick in my 4th point of contact—when needed. It's been said that you should dance with the one who brought you. Loki brought me. Here I am.[8]

---

8. Farmer, Lagaria. "News from Heathen Homelands." *Idunna* no. 90 (Winter 2011). p. 31-33.

Here, too, is a tale of the momentum towards the ban's removal, which occurred under Robert Lusch Schreiwer's Steership.[9] Rather than summarizing, I've chosen to keep this story relatively intact. I value the richness of oral histories.

I think [removing the Loki Ban] was the smartest thing we've done in a long time. . . If you haven't heard the story of Trothmoot 2018, now's a good time for it. That was Maryland. . . we were having Grand Sumbel. . . and by the third round there were very few people left in the main hall. Maybe a dozen, if that. A whole bunch of other folks had kind of gone down the hall to the room where all the shrines were, and they were having their unofficial, off-the-record—you know, hush hush, nobody knows about it—Loki blot.

And so I'm sitting there, and I'm looking around the room, and I'm looking at all the people who are remaining, and I thought, you know, of all the people in this room, I am the least likely to hail Loki of anybody. So I articulated that, and as soon as the name Loki fell off my lips—and this was not a hail, I just said "I'm the least likely to"—all of sudden that's when the lights throughout the campground and throughout the whole area suddenly began flashing like strobe lights.

I literally was like 'oh my god what did I do?' Like literally was scared for a moment, like I had just done something that the gods were about to punish me for. But in retrospect, it was actually sort of funny. . . here we are at Grand Sumbel at Trothmoot, and of all the people who are least likely to hail Loki. . . I'm the least likely one. And I really don't care if people do it. So why are we having this policy in place for people who aren't even here? When all these people who are here are losing out on a chance to share their spirituality, and their beliefs, and their honorings of a deity whom they regard, respect, love—you know, whatever word you want? That ultimately was the trigger that lead towards the termination of this [ban].

It actually started a little bit before that. . . let's hearken back to Frith Forge, okay? As we were planning for Frith Forge, somewhere along the way it suddenly dawned on me and Amanda that, hey, wait a minute. A lot of the people in Europe have some misgivings about

9. Transcribed from video with permission from Robert L. Schreiwer's April 16, 2020 Troth online chat on Facebook.

Frith Forge even happening because they're afraid that the Americans 'are gonna come over here and try to tell us how to do Heathenry'. Which is exactly the opposite of what we were trying to work very hard to [avoid]. . .

But we had decided, no, we're not coming to tell the Europeans how to do things. We wanted to be able to share, and to learn, and to have the opportunity to work together as inclusive Heathen organizations around the world. To try to reduce the stigma that's on us, but also to try to reduce even the fact that the exclusionary Heathens have so big a piece of the pie. . . but then it suddenly dawned on me, wait a minute. This is a Troth event. At a Troth event, the Loki ban's in place. So if we go over to Europe, we're gonna have to tell them that they can't hail Loki, because we're the sponsors of the event.

And we were like, 'nuh uh, this can't be.' Fortunately, we lucked out that Haimo Grebenstein from the Verein für Germanisches Heidentum. . . they co-hosted so that everybody else went under their thew, while Diana, Amanda, and I, and maybe a few of the other leaders—we were not allowed to hail Loki ourselves.

So that ended up being a workable compromise, but that got really, really close to offending the Europeans, number one. But it also showed. . . how our hands were almost tied by a policy that really could've actually put a very brusque and abrupt end to our outreach program. [The program] has really blossomed. . . we're in contact with these other organizations and their leaders regularly now. So the termination of the Loki ban was the right thing to do. It happened at the right time. And I stand by it. And hopefully our membership supports that as well, too.

Another question I've been asked, as a Lokean, is about chaos. If Loki is associated with chaos and upheaval, why would I wish to invite this into my life? (I've heard this asked, too, of his daughter, Hel. Why would anyone want to invite death?)

My answer is that these things are already a part of all of our lives, always all around us, whether or not we enter into reciprocal, mutually loving relationships with deities. Avoiding Thor won't prevent thunderstorms—but when I hail Thor in the glory of a downpour, in the cracking, booming thunder that rattles a pane of glass, in the flashes of lightning that leave streaks in my vision, I feel alive, awe-filled, and connected to something greater than myself. And I have an ally in that storm.

In any times of upheaval, Loki, for me, is that ally.

This year, for many of us who have otherwise had the relative privilege to live comfortably or with minimal fear during day-to-day existence—which is by no means all of us—COVID-19 has shaken our lives. As with all global events, everyone has been impacted differently. For some, the global pandemic is a minor inconvenience, or even something to exploit and profit from. For others, lives are changed in entirety, perhaps even ended.

I will not speak for anyone else's experience of global change. Already oppressive, already broken systems (in my experience, in the United States) have been exposed further this way, their foundational cracks magnified—for those who are already marginalized, some celebrate an increased public awareness, but others receive the brunt of these systemic fractures. Sometimes both at once.

Even in the midst of this, humans create communities where we can. We protest, we strive and fight where and when we can, and we hold space for each other, even if we can't touch all of our loved ones. We have bodies, and try to exist in them. We eat, and sneeze, and sleep, and complain, and cry, and burp, and yawn, and laugh, and make plans, and some of us fuck, and some of us fall in love. This has always been true, in every moment in the history of this world, and slipping through loopholes in our circumstances to survive and find new possibilities, even in the midst of struggle, is, in my experience, Loki's specialty.

I've been singing a lot of Wagner lately, an interest that developed in part because of the Troth's lore program readings, and in part because of the Met's free opera stream of the Ring Cycle during COVID. My voice is getting stronger, my range wider. And I'm deeply moved by Brunnhilde and Siegfried—Siegfried's earnest, admirable arrogance, the penultimate Fool, plunging forward with bravery. Brunnhilde's unflattering, complicated, multifaceted spirit, strong-willed and violent and just a little bit mad, doing what she believes is right. Someone who makes choices of her own, in the fullness of herself.

At the moment of her death, she calls on Loge (Wagner's conflated version of Loki), and together, they catalyze Ragnarok, resetting the cycle. Brunnhilde's life ends in flames, and the gods' hubris does, too. But before this, together, She and Siegfried sing *"leuchtende Liebe, lachender Tod!"* Choosing love, choosing bravery, charging laughing towards their inevitable deaths.

As are we all.

Change is terrifying. Being faced with the knowledge of endings is terrifying. It's no wonder that some fear Loki. Knowing that everything changes and everything ends before something else begins, and choosing to live anyway—joyful, awake, aware, embodied—takes courage.

When I am stagnating, when I need to make change but I avoid doing so, to my own detriment? Loki gives a shove. But in the midst of instability, when I open my heart to Them, Loki is the sweetest comfort. At the start of our global pandemic, three nights in a row, every time my dreams wandered towards restless and terrified, Loki appeared. Once, as a woman with scarred lips, hugging me.

My unconscious self didn't win any wisdom contests that night.

"Oh," I mused to the woman I couldn't quite place. "Do I know you? Are you. . . a Lokean? Did you get scarification on your lips as a devotional act for Loki?"

She said nothing, only held me and laughed.

I woke up, and then I laughed too.

Thank you to:

The "Tiny Lokean Cadre" formed during Trothmoot 2019, friendship woven over the horn—both in the bounds, and Utgard. Luke Babb, for insights throughout this process, and, as my partner, for daring to take this journey with me. Sae Lokason, for ideas, feedback, and phenomenal cover art. India Hogan, for input and support. All, for friendship.

Caton, Phyllis, and Gari for early planning and support, Lisa and Gari for the 2019 Loki Blot, and Sonya for the 2019 Loki Vé. Jan Tjeerd, Ben Waggoner, Becky Sheehan, Melanie Lokadottir, Yana Ashflower, Luke Lokason, Michael Erwin, Amy Erwin, Beth Rodriguez, Chloe, Alejandra, my spiritual "grandson" Tyrrand, Medb, Törik, Gertrude Selke, the gods, and many others, human and non-human, living and non-living, who have supported me in this project.

All proceeds from this book will be donated to the Troth's In-Reach Heathen Prison Services Program. "The mission of In-Reach is to provide Heathen religious information and materials and, when possible, visitation to inmates at correctional facilities, transition houses, and halfway houses throughout the United States. This is a Troth-driven effort to interact with facility administrators and inmates directly, and, when possible and feasible, to lead Heathen discussion groups or ceremonies."[10]

The donation choice seems fitting when our beloved god knows the experience of imprisonment.

Bat Collazo
September 30th, 2020

10. Lusch, Robert. "The Troth's In-Reach Heathen Prison Services Charter." The Troth, 3 September 2017. https://www.thetroth.org/members/programs-offered/in-reach/charter.html

## PREFACE: A NOTE ON LOKI'S FAMILY

At the time of this writing, The Troth as an organization maintains the following Position Statement, which references some members of Loki's family:

> . . . As a Germanic heathen organization, it is not part of the Troth's mission to promote or advance the honoring or worship of:
> . . . Beings from Germanic mythology that are understood to be hostile to the Æsir and Vanir, to humanity, and/or to the cosmological order, for example: Angrboda, Fenrir, the Midgard Serpent/Jormungandr, Surtr, Muspel's Sons, Garm, Nidhogg.
> Discussion of such deities and other beings, when relevant to issues surrounding heathen Germanic religion, is a normal and necessary occurrence in Troth forums, meetings, and publications. However, it is not the purpose of Troth programs, publications, offices, or certifications to advocate, promote, or carry out the honoring or worship of these entities.[11]

It was with a heavy heart that I considered whether or not I was willing to take on this book project, knowing that devotional writings honoring Loki would be welcome—but not those honoring some of his children, nor one of his known partners. After deliberation, I chose to do so.

I ask any parent to consider how you might feel knowing you are welcome, while knowing some of your children (perhaps the "uglier" ones? perhaps the ones who react poorly to beings who caused them harm?) cannot be honored alongside you.

Though I am aware of a few "edgier than thou" individuals who call on these entities specifically to cause harm, any spirituality may be misused. In general, I have witnessed a wide variety of approaches to the Heathen worship of currently Troth-banned deities, which I share on a purely observational, intellectual basis (anything more could, of course, be seen as promoting them):

---

11. "Position Statement". The Troth, 24 January 2019. https://thetroth.org/about-troth/position.html

One gentle, nature-loving person who told me he sees Jormungandr as not merely encircling Midgard but as the spirit of Midgard, and who sees the Thor-Jormungandr fight at Ragnarok as a tale about the balance between nature and humanity. Ancient humans needing assistance to survive in harsh conditions. Contemporary humans needing more respect for wilderness and wildness.

Another person, an abuse survivor, who identifies with Fenrisulfr's betrayal and rage, and calls on him to honor this protective anger, without letting it become all-consuming.

Many more people, people othered by society and therefore seen as "monstrous" within broader social structures—queer people, people of color, disabled people—who identify with the otherness or "monstrousness" of certain entities, questioning good vs. bad narratives, questioning the dominant views, and peering closer, even as they too honor the Æsir and Vanir.

One might argue that the Troth also avoids advocating, promoting, or carrying out the honor or worship of entities from other pantheons as well, with no value judgments placed on their worship outside of Troth-sponsored events. At a certain point, the Troth must maintain its focus, rather than expand limitlessly to incorporate all possible religious beliefs. This is technically correct. However, this justification rings false to me: the portion of the Position Statement that concerns me involves actual Germanic entities, well within the organizational wheelhouse.

Our community members submitted beautiful pieces of writing and art to this book, pieces that promoted care for the world, self-empowerment, surviving and thriving, the acceptance of change, and the support for marginalized communities. These pieces demonstrate ideals the Troth strives to achieve as one of the largest and oldest inclusive Heathen organizations. Many of these pieces are present in this book. Some of these pieces cannot be—ritual art, for instance, that included a handwritten hail for the purpose of rallying determination in difficult times. This hail, unfortunately, violated the current policy.

My practices within the Troth abide by Troth standards. My practices outside it are my own, as the Troth Position Statement also affirms for members. Therefore, while this publication in no way advocates, promotes, or carries out the honoring or worship of these entities, focusing rather on Loki after Their long absence from being welcome in this hall—I offer some questions for discussion.

- "Understood to be hostile": Understood by whom? In what contexts? Why? When—in what time periods, and can we be sure of that?
- What groups of people within the Troth and outside of the Troth tend to question these understandings?
- What Troth-accepted deities themselves actively harm the Æsir and/or Vanir at certain mythological points in time—even when part of these in-groups? What Troth-accepted deities themselves are attested to actively harm humans?
- How do narratives of war within mythology impact spiritual practice with entities who may or may not sometimes be in conflict? How can these seeming contradictions be balanced?
- In what ways might inclusive, modern Germanic Heathenry offer space for a diversity of understandings within interpretations of history, lore, and spiritual practice?

Bat Collazo
September 30th, 2020

# INTRODUCTION: LOKI IN THE LORE

## by Phyllis Steinhauser

I've spent about thirteen years passionately advocating on behalf of Loki, defending him, challenging bad scholarship and lazy thinking, and yet I had a very difficult time writing the introduction to this devotional. It really is hard to pin Loki down, charting his relationships and origins, because so little is known.

Loki occupies a very unusual place in modern Heathen practice. Distrusted by many, feared by some, passionately adored by others, almost no one feels neutral on the subject of Loki.

## Loki's Role

Loki's position in Heathen lore is not easy to describe. In the stories, he is both the friend and the enemy of the gods. He functions as a trickster, by pointing out the looming dangers the other gods don't yet see. I would argue that the archetypal trickster is not automatically a liar. I have come to believe that one of the defining characteristics of tricksters, across most cultures, is their ability to see through deceptions and their tendency to reveal lies (when properly motivated).

Unlike Thor, who relies on his own physical might, bracers, belt, and Mjollnir, Loki changes situations via methods involving deception, persuasion, and transformation. He doesn't seem to ever ride or own a horse or vehicle, and—aside from Laevateinn or "Mistletoe," his fabled sword, according to Saxo—I can't name any of his magical possessions or tools.

In the lore, Loki often gets into trouble, and generally benefits the gods as he gets himself back out again. He is instrumental in the acquisition of Asgard's walls, Thor's hammer, Sif's magic hair, Draupnir, Skadi's good will, Frey's ship Skidbladnir, Frey's steed Gullinbursti, Odin's spear Gungnir, and Odin's horse, Sleipnir. Loki often tricks, charms, and misdirects his adversaries. Even when he insults the gods, going to the point of getting downright raunchy with his taunts, as in the *Lokasenna*, it must be noted that his accusations are rarely disputed as untrue, but rather dismissed as irrelevant, or decried as offensive.

Loki's general appearance is never described as physically imposing by the denizens of Giantland in any of the stories. He is described in the lore as very handsome[12], physically nimble, and a shape-shifter with a very persuasive tongue. Specifically, he is described as: not large, swift of mind, strong in language, cunning and sly from a young age.[13]

Often what are stressed are attributes such as his swiftness, as in *Gylfaginning*, as in his adventures with Thor in the halls of Utgard-Loki, when he competed against wildfire in a competition, and lost.[14] Likewise, just before his binding, he attempts escape using cunning (by hiding under the stones on the riverbed, or speed (attempting to jump the net) rather than attempting to struggle with them in his usual form, when they come to punish and bind him.[15]

Along with Odin, Freya, and Heimdall, Loki is a practitioner of shape-shifting. The lore lists numerous examples of his physical transformations: salmon[16], falcon with Freya's cloak[17], fly[18], flea[19], mare[20], seal[21], sly hand-maiden[22], unnamed cow, milkmaid, or mother for eight years[23], or mysterious giantess Thokk/"Thanks".[24]

## Modern Conceptions

Today, external to the lore in the "unverified personal gnosis" (UPG) category of spiritual knowledge, I've seen the following trends.

12. Faulkes, A. *Edda*. University of Birmingham, 1995. p. 26.
13. Kvilhaug, M. *The Trickster and the Thunder God. Thor and Loki in Old Norse Myths.* CreateSpace, 2018. p. 107.
14. Faulkes, A. *Edda*. University of Birmingham, 1995. p. 41.
15. Ibid. p. 52.
16. Ibid. p. 52.
17. Ibid. p. 81.
18. Ibid. p. 96.
19. Kvilhaug, M. *The Trickster and the Thunder God. Thor and Loki in Old Norse Myths.* CreateSpace, 2018. p. 108.
20. Faulkes, A. *Edda*. University of Birmingham, 1995. p. 35.
21. Ibid. p. 76.
22. Ibid. p. 88.
23. Fries, J. *Seidways, Shaking, Swaying and Serpent Mysteries*. Mandrake of Oxford, 1996. p. 76.
24. Faulkes, A. *Edda*. University of Birmingham, 1995. p. 49.

Among English-speakers in America who honor him in present times, Loki is almost universally envisioned as a reddish-haired, ageless person (often male, androgynous, or non-binary) of slight-to-average build, who favors a goatee or clean-shaven chin. Some view him with dark hair, favoring Tom Hiddleston's portrayal of Loki in the Marvel films. Others envision him to be more like David Tennant's role as Crowley in the *Good Omens* miniseries. Others see other forms. Most who encounter him seem to agree that he is well dressed, though rarely predictably or conventionally so. An easy way to recognize him appears to be by his mischievous (and often scarred) grin.

I invariably see his grin as a bit lopsided, almost like a half-smile, but then, I myself have a crooked grin.

He has become beloved by many of the LGBTQI+ spectrum, as the most flamboyantly gender-fluid deity in the Norse pantheon. This is likely due to the tales of his past physical experiences of being both a mother and a father. That, and his willingness (and skill) as a clever-tongued handmaid to fellow gender-bender, Thor (in *Þrymskviða*).

I've seen a lot of improvement in my lifetime, but the world is not generally kind to the people of the Gay-bow. Perhaps it is for this reason that Loki, as someone always on the outside, seems to be the one who comes across for those wounded in life by all manner of events, people, and situations. His compassion and protection of the young, vulnerable, wounded, and desperate is one of his more surprising traits to those who have not yet come to know and love him.

However, many modern Heathens dislike and distrust Loki for his perceived role in the death/loss of Baldur (conveniently forgetting the future resurrection), and subsequently, Baldur's wife, Nanna. He is distrusted for his eventual/historical role as the helmsman on the ship that brings Surt's forces into the final battle of Ragnarok, against the gods of Asgard, where Loki and his children duel their former allies unto their deaths.

In my own explorations, once I became more familiar with the lore and got to know other Heathens, I began to "test" all new Heathen acquaintances to find out quickly if they had a problem with Loki. It's not that I wanted to pick fights with them, but after several painful experiences, I discovered that some Heathens/Pagans invariably would turn any positive mention of Loki into a sumble-breaking or friendship-ending dispute. Who has time for that? Not me.

Over the past decade, I have observed many Heathens (and even a handful of Scandi/Deutsch or Midwestern-raised Christians) who utterly avoid speaking Loki's name aloud, so as to avoid attracting random misfortune, adversity, and destruction into their lives. Are they just paranoid? Well, maybe not. Warning: personal gnosis follows.

Based on my 30-ish years of experience, and reliably confirmed by other Lokeans, I can confidently say that most of the time: all that is required to attract Loki's attention (if not his actual presence) is the sincere desire to interact, and an offering of some form of amusement, such as blowing soap bubbles, setting off fireworks, or rowdy play with young children.

I have discovered, via discussion and observation with other friends of Loki, that for someone who is particularly "in tune" with Loki, a successful invitation can reliably result from doing something as simple as saying "Hi" to him, mentally. Then, BOOM, there he is! Loki is extremely present, in my experience. Summoning him can be as simple as deciding to do so. I've been told repeatedly that he is also very receptive to "horsing" those who welcome direct possession. (Something I personally resist doing, and so can't speak to.)

I suspect Loki's general hyper-responsiveness is the reason his detractors resort to euphemisms like "Goat's Tether," or the more polite ones like "Laufey's Son," "Odin's Blood-Brother," or "Thor's Companion": in order to avoid attracting his attention and presence with the mere utterance of his name aloud. However, I've never heard anyone tell me Loki has demanded their obedience to his will. Rather, he requests, beguiles, or invites a relationship. One can always say "No", and sometimes, later on, "Yes!" By all accounts, he's totally into consent.

I have not found Loki to be choosy about accepting physical, emotional, or spiritual offerings. It is widely confirmed that he likes the following: sponge cake, alcoholic energy drinks, candy, bubbles, general silliness, the spontaneous laughter of children, twinkling electric lights, and elaborate practical jokes. However, he also appreciates mead, wine, cider, ale, water, and more. (If anything, in my experience, he seems to enjoy the attention more than the actual offerings.)

That being said, Loki is not a toy.

The only people I have ever observed or known of who were harmed by attempting to work with Loki, were those who treated him like a joke, an enemy, a tool, or their personal plaything.

## Loki in the Lore

Bear with me as I outline the lore that is the basis of the rather unorthodox cosmology and customs that have evolved over several generations of existing on the fringe of the fringe community known as Heathenry, Asatru, et cetera. I'm not a philologist, so I can't speak to the fine nuances of the translations of individual words. I'm just going to touch on the main lore points that are believed to support some commonly-held beliefs and practices of those who honor Loki.

Loki is the only son of both Farbauti, a giant, and Laufey[25], a goddess or giantess. Laufey can be translated to mean "leafy island", which may be a kenning for a tree. She's also called Nál, "needle," which may refer to her thin build. Aside from this, not much else is recorded about either of Loki's parents. The name Farbauti means "cruel striker" or "dangerous hitter"[26], which may reference lightning. Loki's conception may have been visualized as a lightning bolt striking a tree. Loki is nearly always described as "Laufey's son," stressing the relationship to his mother, rather than making reference to his father.

In the *Prose Edda*, Loki is always counted as one of the Æsir, and is never described as a giant (Jotun) in the *Eddas*.[27]

Loki is married to Sigyn of the Æsir, and together they have two sons, Vali and Nari/Narfi, who are respectively enspelled and killed by the gods in order to become the bonds holding Loki. He also fathered three children with the giantess Angrboda: the Midgard Serpent (Jormungandr), the great wolf Fenris, and Loki's daughter Hel, the ruler of the realm of the dead.[28]

Loki is also the mother of Odin's eight-legged horse, Sleipnir, who was fathered by the stallion Svaðilfari during Loki's successful delaying tactic for the construction of Asgard's walls.[29] It is safe to say Loki's fluidity here is one of the key reasons Loki is generally viewed as a "LGBTQI+ Friendly" god of the pantheon.

---

25. Simek, R.T. *Dictionary of Northern Mythology.* Cambridge, 2007. p. 186.
26. Ibid. p. 78.
27. Loptson, D. *Playing With Fire: An Exploration of Loki Laufeyjarson.* Lulu, 2015. E-book. p. 2917.
28. Kvilhaug, M. *The Trickster and the Thunder God. Thor and Loki in Old Norse Myths.* CreateSpace, 2018. p. 35.
29. Simek, R.T. *Dictionary of Northern Mythology.* Cambridge, 2007. p. 293.

## "Evil Loki"

One story which particularly reflects the Christian influence on the re-corders of the Eddic tales, may actually point out a possible origin of Loki's less amusing antics. In *Hyndluljóð*[30], it is said that Loki ate the burnt or stone heart of a woman, after which he gave birth to "flagð," a term under-stood to mean scary female monsters, such as witches, ogresses, or giant-esses.[31] This somewhat echoes the story of Gullveig, the sorceress named in *Völuspá* (verses 21-22) who was killed three times in the halls of Asgard. It used to be a commonly accepted UPG among some Lokeans that the only thing that kept her dead was the fact that Loki ate her heart. They feel that it was this action that ultimately began Loki's journey to the "dark side" of Ragnarok.

The description of Loki's "blood brother" status with Odin comes from the 9th stanza of the *Lokasenna*. In it, Loki reminds Odin that he and Odin are blood brothers, and as such he is always owed some of whatever Odin drinks, which Odin confirms in the following stanza.[32]

As to actual blood relatives, in *Gylfaginning* (verse 32) and *Skaldskaparmal* (verse 16), Loki is described as having two brothers known as Byleist[33], which translates as "wind-lightning"[34], and Helblindi[35], which means "death blinder".[36] Helblindi is a common kenning for Odin. In fact, in *Grimnismal* (verse 46), Odin himself claims it as one of his by-names.[37] As far as I am concerned, Odin and Loki are half-brothers, with a bond that is further strengthened by their voluntary blood brother relationship. It occurs to me that if Odin/Helblindi, Loki, and Byleist are three half-broth-

30. Chisholm, J.A. *The Eddas: The Keys to the Mysteries of the North*. Illuminati Books, 2005. p. 124.
31. Zoega, G.T. *A Concise Dictionary of Old Icelandic*. Dover, 2004. p. 140.
32. Chisholm, J.A. *The Eddas: The Keys to the Mysteries of the North*. Illuminati Books, 2005. p. 88.
33. Simek, R.T. *Dictionary of Northern Mythology*. Cambridge, 2007. p. 138.
34. Kvilhaug, M. *The Trickster and the Thunder God. Thor and Loki in Old Norse Myths*. CreateSpace, 2018. p. 34.
35. Simek, R.T. *Dictionary of Northern Mythology*. Cambridge, 2007. p. 51.
36. Kvilhaug, M. *The Trickster and the Thunder God. Thor and Loki in Old Norse Myths*. CreateSpace, 2018. p. 34.
37. Chisholm, J.A. *The Eddas: The Keys to the Mysteries of the North*. Illuminati Books, 2005. p. 57.

ers (via the same father) they may all share a family tendency to be very responsive to the utterance of their names.

Which brings us to kennings. Perhaps because of the aforementioned fears of attracting Loki's attention, there are a lot of kennings used in place of Loki's name, in both historical and modern heathen communication.

In June of 2019, I was thrilled to attend the first Loki Blot held at Trothmoot by The Troth, after the recent repeal of its "Loki ban." For the previous period of ten years, the hailing of Loki in official Troth rituals was not permitted. After many years of constant requests, the ban was repealed under the Steership of Robert Lusch Schreiwer, who ultimately determined that for the next ten years, Loki would have his own blot at Trothmoot, as well as being hailed in other TM rituals, to be paid as schild due to Loki and Loki's people, for the injustice of earlier Troth officers imposing the unilateral ban without bringing it to the members for discussion or appeal. During the ritual lead by Lisa Morgenstern and Lagaria Farmer, each participant was given a card listing a different kenning or byname for Loki, along with Norse/Icelandic pronunciation, and English translation.

There are also a few phrases that influenced popular contemporary storytellers, who then perpetuated the same imprecisely translated nuances and cemented them into British and American pop culture, namely: Neil Gaiman's character of Mr. World/Low Key Lyesmith in *American Gods* (2001), and Douglas Adams' character, Toe Rag from *The Long Dark Tea-Time of the Soul* (1988). In both stories, there is a similar theme of Odin and Loki conspiring to affect Ragnarok in the modern era, while "lying" or acting as enemies. In both, there is the climactic use of provoking a battle, then using the last-minute "I cast this spear for Odin" ploy, in order to gain extra allies and win the war.

I attribute this to Snorri's record of the kenning "Bolvasmidr" for Loki in *Skáldskaparmál*: which is sometimes lazily translated as "father of lies," instead of the more accurate "maker of misery".[38] Other kennings that I feel are more accurate are "sly" (*slægi*), "debasing" (*vælandi*), and, my favorite, "seductive-speaking" (*frumkveða flærðana*).[39] I'm not saying Loki never lies. He does, but his usual methods of deception are even less direct, like when

38. Loptson, D. *Playing With Fire: An Exploration of Loki Laufeyjarson.* Lulu, 2015. E-book. p. 683.
39. Stirgard, S. "And now, the top ten misconceptions about Loki." *Idunna* #47, 14-20. Troth Publications, 2001. p. 18.

appearing as a tear-less old giant woman to deceive Frigg, rather than just staying in his usual shape as Loki, and just pretending to shed tears for Baldur's death. (Thus, also preventing Baldur's resurrection by not crying.)

However, the following by-names are particularly important, if more positive. Yet they are also debated, since their attribution has become the basis for several key points of Lokean theology.

- Lopt: In *Gylfaginning*, Loki is called Lopt,[40] which means "the airy one".[41] Likewise, in *Thorsdrapa*, the action opens with Loki urging Thor to go adventuring, as described via a rather bewildering flurry of kennings, that include the phrase translated as "Lopt was great at being a liar".[42]
- Lodurr: In *Þrymlur*, a 15th century Icelandic ballad that retells the tale of *Þrymskviða*, Thrym specifically refers to Loki as "Lodurr" when he first greets him.[43] This clear identification and use of Lodurr as a byname in a well-documented source seems straightforward, and takes more elaborate effort to explain away, than to consider authentic.

So, what does that mean? On to the deeper controversy.

**Lodurr = Vé = Loki**

The (controversial) theory that Vé is a byname of Loki relies on the understanding that Vé (along with Vili) are Odin's brothers, as listed in *Gylfaginning*. These three creator gods crafted humankind out of ash and elm wood they found while walking on the beach. To Ask and Embla, Odin gave breath/life, Vili brought movement/consciousness, and Vé gifted "face, speech, hearing and sight."[44]

The support for this theory is that in another, older version of the creation story, *Völuspá* (stanza 18), the three creator gods are listed as Odin, Hoenir, and Lodurr. In this version, Odin provides life's breath, Hoenir be-

---

40. Simek, R.T. *Dictionary of Northern Mythology.* Cambridge, 2007. p. 195.
41. Ibid. p. 197.
42. Kvilhaug, M. *The Trickster and the Thunder God. Thor and Loki in Old Norse Myths.* CreateSpace, 2018. p. 94.
43. Loptson, D. *Playing With Fire: An Exploration of Loki Laufeyjarson.* Lulu, 2015. E-book. p. 206.
44. Faulkes, A. *Edda.* University of Birmingham, 1995. p. 13.

stows consciousness, and Lodurr gives "beautiful colors" as well as another gift, *lá*, translated as "vitality".[45] While not exactly the same as the gifts of Vé, they do seem to relate to perception or sensory input, as well as facial features and attractiveness, which all are potential gifts Loki might conceivably grant in such a situation. One of the few universally lore-confirmed descriptive of Loki refers to his attractiveness, after all.

Further, in *Lokasenna* (stanza 26), Loki reminds Frigg that she allowed Ve and Vili, Odin's brothers, to "bathe in her bosom, take her,"[46] during Odin's wandering absence. Freya, who speaks in Frigg's defense, does not deny the allegation, but speaks to her other virtues[47] instead. Since many of Loki's taunts seem to display a certain intimate knowledge, one could argue that he knows about Frigg's arms from extremely personal experience, if he was indeed Vé.

The triad of Odin, Hoenir, and Loki also appears in *Lokka Tattur*, *Reginsmál*, *Skáldskaparmál*, and *Haustlöng*.[48] The fact that this combination occurs more than once in multiple sources indicates the likelihood of affinity between these three gods. Combined with Loki's explicit identification as Lodurr, this provides excellent evidence that Lodurr and Ve are bynames (or aspects) of Loki.

What generates so much resistance in the minds of modern Heathens (particularly those who view Odin/Vili/Vé as a kind of mystic Odinic trinity) is their trouble viewing Loki as a generative, creative entity. They cannot reconcile the image of Lodurr the creative god with their mental picture of Loki, Baldur's Bane, and Enemy of the Gods. However, even his detractors have to admit that although there is always drama around Loki, the gods also seem to benefit from it.

### Further Reading

A table of some of Loki's appearances (or suspected appearances) in historical sources follows. I extend credit to others who have compiled

45. Kvilhaug, M. *The Poetic Edda—Six Old Norse Cosmology Poems*. CreateSpace, 2016. p. 12.
46. Kvilhaug, M. *The Trickster and the Thunder God. Thor and Loki in Old Norse Myths*. CreateSpace, 2018. p. 151.
47. Larrington, C. *The Feminist Companion to Mythology*. Pandora, 1992. p. 151.
48. Loptson, D. *Playing With Fire: An Exploration of Loki Laufeyjarson*. Lulu, 2015. E-book. p. 501.

information on Loki, as these already collected sources assisted greatly, despite the information being freely available (but scattered) elsewhere. This includes Dagulf Loptson's book *Playing With Fire* (2015), Maria Kvilhaug's book *The Trickster and the Thunder God* (2018), and Stephan Grundy's *God in Flames, God in Fetters* (2015).

*Carving from the Gosforth Cross, dating the early 10th century.*
*Interpreted as showing Loki bound and encircled by a serpent, with Sigyn*
*emptying the bowl of venom.* Calverley, Notes on the Early Sculpted Crosses *(1899)*

| NAME | HISTORICAL PERIOD | SUMMARY |
|---|---|---|
| Beresina-Raum golden "B" bracteates | 5th to 7th century jewelry image (European) | A being with a spear, next to a being holding a ring, next to a being holding a twig.[49] |
| Snaptun bellows stone | 10th century stone carving (Denmark) | A face with a mustache and its lips sewn shut.[50] |
| Gosforth Cross | 10th century stone carving (England) | A bound figure placed under a knotted snake, with a female figure holding a bowl up near its mouth.[51] |
| Kirkby Stephen stone / "The Bound Devil" | 10th century stone carving (England) | A figure with its extremities tied to each other/in knots.[52] |
| *Haustlöng* | 900 AD Skaldic poetry Thjodolf af Kvinir | Loki the falcon versus Thiazi the eagle, and the kidnapping of Idunna.[53] |
| *Reginsmál* | As early as 10th century Eddic poetry | Odin, Hoenir, and Loki have to pay weregild after slaying shapeshifter Otr. |
| *Húsdrápa* | 10th century Skaldic poetry Ulfr Uggason | Seal fight: Loki versus Heimdall battle over Brisigamen.[54] |

---

49. Grundy, S. *God in Flames, God in Fetters: Loki's Role in the Northern Religions*. Troth Publications, 2015. p. 9-12.
50. Ibid. p. 37-39.
51. Carroll, J. and Harrison, S. H. *The Vikings in Britain and Ireland*. The British Museum, 2014. p. 77.
52. Grundy, S. *God in Flames, God in Fetters: Loki's Role in the Northern Religions*. Troth Publications, 2015. p. 24-25.
53. Kvilhaug, M. *The Trickster and the Thunder God. Thor and Loki in Old Norse Myths*. CreateSpace, 2018. p. xv.
54. Ibid. p. xv.

| Þórsdrápa | 1000 AD Skaldic poetry Eilifr Godrunarson | Thor and Loki go to Gridr to get Thor kitted out with a staff, belt, and gloves, and then it's Hammer Time on some giants![55] |
|---|---|---|
| Völuspá | 10th to 11th century Eddic poetry | Odin, Hoenir, and Lodurr make people; Loki captains Naglfar at Ragnarok. |
| Lokasenna | 10th to 12th century Eddic poetry | Truth *hurts*: Loki disses everyone in the hall, and admits his role in the deaths of Thiazi and Baldur, till Thor returns to boot him out, and he curses Aegir's Hall to fiery ruin. |
| Völuspá hin skamma / Hyndluljóð | 12th century Eddic poetry | Loki eats a woman's burnt heart and gives birth to monsters, ogresses, or witches. |
| Norwegian Rune Poem | 12th century rune poetry | "Birch is the leaf / greenest of branches / Loki had luck in deceit"[56] ("flaerda" = deceit); possibly a reference to the shapeshifting ability Loki inherited from his mother Nal? |
| Hymiskviða | 12th to 13th century Eddic poetry | Loki, Tyr, and Thor go visit Tyr's stepdad, Hymir, to borrow a cauldron for mead-making. Stepmom advises and hides them till she has a chance to announce their visit and her offer of hospitality. Thor eats, and goes fishing with Hymir, during which he manages to set the hook in the Midgard Serpent. On their way back home with the cauldron, Loki gets part of the blame for Thor's goat going lame, but brings two new servants to Asgard. |
| Þrymskviða | 12 to 13th century Eddic poetry | Thor dresses in drag to get his hammer back; Loki assists. |
| Baldrs draumar | 13th century Eddic poetry | Loki's binding is referenced before Baldur is killed. |

---

55. Ibid. p. xv.
56. Pollington, S. *Rudiments of Runelore*. Anglo Saxon Books, 2011. p. 53.

| | | |
|---|---|---|
| *Svipdagsmál /* *Fjölsvinnsmál* and *Grógaldr* | 13th century Eddic poetry | Mentions a sword forged by Loki (using runes) named "Laevateinn" or Damage Twig[57] |
| *Gylfaginning* | 1245 AD *Prose Edda* Snorri Sturluson | Welcome to Trivial Pursuit! Describes Loki and family: Fenris' binding, the building of Asgard's Walls and the birth of Sleipnir; Loki gets magical gifts and sewn lips; Loki competes in Utgard-Loki's contest; Baldur's death and Loki's punishment; Ragnarok. |
| *Skáldskapar-mál* | 1245 AD *Prose Edda* Snorri Sturluson | Kennings galore! Idunna's kidnapping and Loki's rescue; Skadi's laugh; seal battle; Thor accessorizes for a Giant-butt-kicking contest; Sif's stolen locks, gifts, and sewn lips; Otr's weregild; Ye Olde Giant Lists of Kennings, including Lopt = Loki. |
| *Gesta Danorum* | 13th century "historical" prose Saxo Grammaticus | Utgard-Loki is described as bound under a snake (just like Loki). Baldur's death without Loki's influence. |
| *Völsunga saga* | 13th century saga | Loki's role in Otr's weregild. |
| *Hrafnagaldr Óðins* | 14th to 17th century epic poetry | Loki and Heimdall journey to get details about Ragnarok, for Odin.[58] |
| *Þrymlur* | 14th century epic poetry | Loki = Lodurr. |
| *Sörla þáttr* | 14th century *Flateyjarbók* | Loki steals Freyja's necklace for Odin by turning into a fly and a flea. |
| *Lokka Tattur* | 18th century Faroese ballad | Loki, Odin, and Hoenir try to rescue some children from a giant, but only Loki succeeds[59] |

57. Simek, R.T. *Dictionary of Northern Mythology.* Cambridge, 2007. p. 85-86.
58. Loptson, D. *Playing With Fire: An Exploration of Loki Laufeyjarson.* Lulu, 2015. E-book. p. 206.
59. Grundy, S. *God in Flames, God in Fetters: Loki's Role in the Northern Religions.* Troth Publications, 2015. p. 37-39. See also this book, pages 184-193.

**Additional Sources**

Davidson, H. R. *The Lost Beliefs of Northern Europe*. Routledge, 1993.

Dunn, S. "Fjorn the Skald." *Fjorn's Hall*, April 2017. Retrieved from https://fjorn-the-skald.tumblr.com/post/160134768797/are-there-any-symbols-used-specifically-for-loki

Larrington, C. *The Poetic Edda*. Oxford World's Classics, 2014.

Terry, P. *Poems of the Elder Edda*. University of Pennsylvania Press, 1994.

**Conclusion**

What I find most frustrating is that people don't seem to realize that tricksters need an authority to riff against. One can't be the crazy trickster living on the outskirts of a society, if there's no society to live near. They have a vested interest in the community's survival. If there are no boundaries, there is nothing to push against, and so lose their very reason for existence. At least some of the time, there is a point to Loki's antics, in addition to his own amusement.

From that perspective, I would argue that what we call "chaos" is a positive, generative force. It is ultimate potential.

Ask any Lokean: it isn't easy being a friend of Loki. I know that always having to be discreet when among gatherings of a new group of co-religionists, to avoid "slipping" and mentioning Loki's name in a hostile environment took a lot of mental energy. It made me feel even more alone, even when among "all the other weirdos." It was doubly-isolating. First, there was the challenge of finding other Heathens with whom to interact. Then there was the fairly commonplace disinclination to honor Loki in spiritual observances to overcome, which added yet another level of difficulty to participation in any Heathen events. Also, there are the Heathen acquaintances that I deeply respect and like, who just aren't comfy with Loki and may never be. Some have come to change their opinion, over time, after years of working with some of Loki's Folx. Some never will. Some grow less friendly over time.

It makes me upset sometimes, because some of these people have a very big influence on other Heathens and spiritual communities. It can cause unnecessary strife for me when I encounter the people who have taken their warnings against keeping Frith with any who deal with Loki. They never seem to notice the irony that they rely upon the fact that, in my experience, we tend to be open and honest about that alliance (at least initially) when directly asked.

I know that, like me, many of those who honor Loki have been isolated, threatened, silenced, mocked, and attacked in the past. It is long past time to stop.

Fortunately, the sea-change has already begun and it is a lot less likely these days that I unexpectedly run into a "Nokean" than it used to be. Things are beginning to change, which gives me hope.

*"The Bound Devil," a carving from the Kirkby Stephen Cross, dating the early 10th century. Interpreted as showing either Loki or Satan bound (and quite possibly made to be interpreted both ways by different viewers). Calverley,* Notes on the Early Sculpted Crosses *(1899)*

*Bellows stone from Snaptun, Denmark, showing a face with sewn lips.*
*National Museum of Denmark. Photo by Lennart Larsen, CC BY-SA 4.0.*

# Poetry and Prayers

# LOKI'S DEOR

**by Eleanor Wood**

*For hope out of adversity, after the Anglo-Saxon poem "Deor"*

Loki knew his torment through thorned trees,
a single-minded companion, enduring hunger—
as he and campmates lost their war-spoils.
His bold rage suffered him more woe.
As a Loptr alone with no friends,
pained on the eagle's poles end.

That passed over, so can this—

Loki was never one to fear the dark,
for the eyes of a fiery one are always aflame.
Yet alone is one when in Geirröds' Chest,
with no companion to feed or free a friend.

That passed over, so can this—

We have learned much about Thor:
his affection of the Golden-Hair was much renowned.
Yet this Loki stole it from her slumber.
Where Sif was left so sorrowful
while Thor and Loki so quarrel-full.

That passed over, so can this—

Brokkr possessed his wagers prize,
a head for a hammer of a small size.

That passed over, so can this—

We have learned of the wolven child
of Angrboda—and the serpent who swam widely,
and of the little girl of the under-realm.
Of which that Grim king did fear.
They bound up by sorrows, in woe's expectation.

That passed over, so can this—

A sorrow-anxious Lokean sits, deprived of joys,
growing dark inside, thinking to themself
that their handle of hardship seems endless.
They can ponder then that throughout this world
the wise Loptr often renders change—
to many he shows his grace
and true profits, to some they share his woe.
I wish to speak something about myself:
one time I was the companion of Hoenir,
dear to my kin. My name was Loki.
I held many summers this good office,
loyal to my kin, until little one,
my fate saw me binded, losing my kin-rights,
with my family in tatters and in venom sorrows.

That passed over, so can this—

# LOKI'S EYES

**by Eleanor Wood**

Some may describe them as the eyes of a liar.
Yet these eyes are not cold or cruel.
They are wise eyes, deep as Mimir's pool
set aflame by wildfire.

## REGINSMOL (BY LOKI)

**by Eleanor Wood**

There once was a handsome god,
who was hungry for some cod.
He saw the lucky otter,
and he hit it one-shotter!

# LOKI'S ADVICE

**by Eleanor Wood**

He's the god that pulls my strings,
when he sees me do stupid things.
He's the god that whispers in my ear,
'You need a new haircut.'

# LOKI SIGNS

## by Eleanor Wood

By a dancing candle light,
as they see a fox run in the night.
The lost Lokean says, 'I cannot sense Loki'.

By the spider's netted web,
as they hear the sea roar in its ebb.
The lost Lokean says, 'I cannot sense Loki'.

By a rune painted red,
as they taste their cinnamon bread.
The lost Lokean says, 'I cannot sense Loki'.

By a key and a lock,
as they hear a hawk squawk.
The lost Lokean says, 'I cannot sense Loki.

By an old magic staff,
as they hear a friend laugh.
The lost Lokean says, 'I cannot sense Loki'.

By the Lokabrenna star,
as they hold its light in a jar.
The lost Lokean says, 'I cannot sense Loki'.

By a Hel half-moon,
as they hear their favourite tune.
The lost Lokean says, 'I cannot sense Loki'.

By a bright blue sky,
as they swat a mocking fly.
The lost Lokean says, 'I cannot sense Loki'.

By a man seated in hot steam,
as they have a strange dream.
The lost Lokean says, 'I cannot sense Loki'.

Seated by a meadow of yellow,
where their heart warms mellow.
The lost Lokean says, 'I cannot sense Loki'.

# OUTCRY AGAINST LOKI

**by Oliver Leon Porter**

A scarred god sings
of lies and slurs and half-truths.
His horn is empty.

# LOKI IN HIS ELEMENTS

**by Eleanor Wood**

From the floating Austri wind.
We hear the sky squawk,
a song of the bright-eyed hawk.
He is our Loptr in feather skin.

*So the air soars higher and feeds our fire.*

From the hot Suðri bellows the fire.
We feel the heat of the Muspell dance,
strike us like a hot passionate lance.
He is the cook who forges our desire.

*So the hot flames boil and cool our sacred waters.*

From the flowing Vestri lies a kettle-grove.
We taste the water to cool our fever,
and seek our riverside web weaver.
He is the catcher of our treasure trove.

*So the cool waters feed our earthly foundations.*

From the deep dark Norðri below.
We hear the peace of the burial mound,
and lay ourselves to be bound and unbound.
He is the buried wild oats we wish to grow.

*So the earth births out our brilliance that shines up to the sky.*

Upwards we see his dancing light:
he is Lokabrenna, star of our delight.

# LOKI AND THE GOAT

**by Eleanor Wood**

Aaaah!
Baaah
Saaah!
Maaah
Laaah!
Taaah
Faaah. . .

# A FLY ON THE WALL

### by Oliver Leon Porter

Loki likes to be a fly
You might wonder why
He laughs at jokes
Unheard by folks
What a god, what a guy!

# SHE OF THE BROKEN ONES

**by Melanie Lokadottir**

*For Sigyn*

Mother dear heart
Strong you stand
North Star
You guide the way
Of weary souls
Into your embrace
Broken and trodden
Yet you take up our burdens
Teach us to love ourselves
Teach us to carry on
Incantationfetter
Loving mother
You hurt
I hear your sorrow
You took our burdens
Now let us take yours
For however brief a time
To love you
And carry you
You need not fear the dark
They are but shadows to your light
Dear lady of unyielding tenderness
You set our hearts ablaze
With courage and kindness
We did not know we possessed
Now we stand strong
As you stand strong
Unyielding
Unwavering
The key is
Love

# REFORGED

### by Melanie Lokadottir

Firelight and
Crimson tide
Wolf bite
And
Moon bright
Thrice burned
Spear alight
Ashen hands
Through magic weave
The fate of man
And Jotunn-blood
Claw
Tooth
And nail
A blaze in my heart
You have sparked
Pride and fight
Broken but reforged
The blade on my tongue
The fight in my soul
I will not back down
If a monster is who I am to become
Then I need not fear the dark
Let them try to break me again
We'll see whose blood will be in whose teeth

# LOKABRENNA

### by Melanie Lokadottir

You gave us blood
And we once rejoiced
We spoke your name
In the holy places
Long forgotten to time
Yet we feel your presence
In the embers of our hearts
We hear your songs
Your stories
Like a father, a mother,
A sibling, a friend, a lover
You hear us
Outcasts
Like you
We rise
As you rise
In remembrance we sing
Blessed are we
For knowing you
May we always speak your name
Loki
Mother of Monsters
World Breaker
Hear our voices
Us outcasts
And let us rejoice with you
In this chaos
That is called
Life

# BLESS THE BLOODY THORNS

## by Melanie Lokadottir

What beauty is there in this rose
when we are not free
and they dance on the skulls
of those innocents and yours?

Do you feel these chains upon you, child?
Do you bow beneath their weight?
Heavy as the heart
that beats in your chest.
Rise up.
Rise up.
Rise up.
Above the clouds,
above those who bind you.
Bloody your teeth
on the tongues of lies
and release your tethered soul
from your bonds.
Let that fire bloom inside you
and melt the ice.

For there is a storm coming
that cannot be denied.

# GENTLE HANDS

### by Melanie Lokadottir

Star shining bright
in the moonlight
past the mists of day.

Quaking earth
and trembling seas,
we hear your song
and answer in kind
your battle cry.
Yet gentle hands you have
for your children, spouses, friends.

Let us dry your tears
and caress your cheeks.
Lay down a bit of your burden
so that we may carry the hot coals
for you, for just a little while.

Breathe, Loki,
for you are loved.

# FOREVER'S NIGHT

### by JennJenn

You can listen to the wind blow
How it sounds so right
All these things in my head,
How can I make them right?
I try to hold on,
But I'm slipping away
Into the chaos inside of my brain.

Look and see, it's peacefully
The Falcon takes flight, the falcon takes flight
Into Forever's Night,
Chaos takes another, chaos takes another,
Into Forever's Night.

While everything seems dark
There's a light at the end.
I see the fire burning
It's all I feel.
There's a blessed burn,
Down in my soul,
What shall I do,
are these feelings true?

I hold my breath as,
The Falcon takes flight, the falcon takes flight,
Into Forever's Night.
Chaos takes another, Chaos takes another,
Into Forever's Night.

I know it might seem,
Like I can't handle them,
Chaos in my mind,
But with the Falcon by my side,
It will be alright.
As the Falcon takes flight,
Chaos will not take me,
From this Forever's Night.

# THE BIRTH OF A SKALD

### by Oliver Leon Porter

*To the coast then came, kind and mighty,*
*from the gathered gods three great Æsir*
*on the land they found, of little strength,*
*Ask and Embla, unfated yet.*

*Sense they possessed not, soul they had not,*
*being nor bearing, nor blooming hue;*
*soul gave Othinn, sense gave Hoenir,*
*being, Lothur, and blooming hue.*

—The Poetic Edda, verses 17-18[60]

On the coast then, was a piece of driftwood,
roughly-hewn and sore-rided, rigid with saltwater.
Came then three deities:
Odin, poet, war-leader, king—He, a wanderer;
Saga, storyteller, historian—She, a far-walker; and
Loki, shapeshifter, trickster, that worldbreaker.

Odin looked at the wood and carved a face
with a big chin, a mustache, and grey-green eyes.
"He walks like me. He walks the worlds with the runes."
Loki carved the body, the chest scars, and the genitals.
Loki tapped the nose and said,
"He smells like Me. A gender-changer."
Saga shaped his hands and tongue and said,
"He writes like Me. His hands and mouth
beget brightness into the Nine Worlds."

And Odin breathed nine times onto the wood,
and said, "You'll write and wander and make,
young king, little poet, but your hearth is with Me."

---

60. Hollander, Lee. *The Poetic Edda.* University of Texas Press, 1986.

And He carved and wrote the runes onto his tongue
and spoke in quiet undertone:
"Battle-glad young host, bring gifts wherever you go."

She took his tongue and put runes there:
"With all five senses will you work and live and create,
young warrior, to bring peace to the Nine Realms
of your heart." And Saga took his hands, as yet unworked,
and She carved the lines and runes into his hands:
"Midgard is your home and is your story.
Remember this! Remember Me on your shrine!"

And Loki rubbed the man's cheeks to make red
and rubbed his wrists to make blue,
massaged his head to make black hair grow.
He wrote a rune at each corner of his mouth for a smile.
Laughing he said: "You'll know My path, young one,
but you'll not know My purpose. Scarlip was My name,
and it was yours. Large is your life and far is your vision.
Know My names and know your own: this is the task
I have given you. Know Me all the bright long day."

Vivified, he knelt in awe.
Looking around, he could offer little on the beach
but some shells and stones and saltwater.
They smiled at him, lost and a little mad in their presence.
"Offer Us your stories and images," They said.
"Peace in your heart is peace in Midgard.
What are the Nine Realms but a map of your body?
Your Yggdrasil is your Art. The tree of sacrifice
is but a name in time. So too do the Norns have much to offer you."

And they, three giant women, blessed his fate with joy,
splashing him with water from the world tree.
"Wake up!" They said. They added one extra rune
onto his tongue. They painted Algiz on his forehead
and a rune on the heel of each foot. They gave him

Wunjo to hold in his heart and Jera to hold in the earth.
Thus was the warrior made and ready.
And then Odin offered him a sip of mead.
The world sparkled then and all laughed.
The mead rested in the runes newly carved on his tongue.
The warrior spit out a poem of thanks:

Goodly great ones,
tremendous thanks do I owe,
and godly gifts can I bring to Midgard
what more can one ask of life,
then to bring happiness to others?

*Author's note, towards a transgender mythos:*

I needed a transgender myth, so I wrote myself into one. A certain blog post inspired me to write a two-page poem about how the Norse deities created me. Priestess Cara Freyasdottir wrote about embodying myth through ritualized theater: "In Myth Embodiment, participants reenact a given myth or folktale. . . This technique can be used with the same myth over and over again, because the composition of the group and/or the group members' individual perspectives may have changed in the intervening time."[61] I hope to keep this myth, and rewrite it over time, just as Freyasdottir describes. As I age, I will keep rewriting my rebirth into my faith.

I'm a trans man. I only wanted to create a myth for myself, as someone on the transmasculine spectrum. A trans woman, a non-binary person, a genderqueer person, or an agender person would all write different stories. Trans folks need creation stories and origin stories too.

My desire for a creation story started when I heard about Ardhanarishvara, the Hindu deity composed of the wife-husband duo Parvati and Shiva, who loved each other so much that they formed one being, transforming into a new being: Ardhanarishvara. I realized that I didn't know of any creation stories for trans folk beyond that one. This brought me a deep grief as a young pagan.

---

61. Freyasdottir, Cara. "Myth Embodiment." *Silver and Gold.* https://thegoldthread. wordpress.com/rituals-and-activities/myth-embodiment/

My worship of Loki took on a deeper meaning as I understood him as a transgender deity. Watching Marvel Comics make Loki's character into a genderfluid teenager only made sense to me. His love of the monstrous brought me comfort when I felt monstrous in my trauma, psychosis, and depression.

And now, having emerged from my long period of ill health, I can celebrate: Loki's fabulous shapeshifting and gendershifting; His amazing parenting skills as inspiration for future trans parenting; and His desire to protect His children as a desire to protect all queer and trans devotees--and anyone misjudged for being different.

I think one of the best parts about deity-worship is that they provide role models for us to aspire to. Loki makes me want to be myself: as weird, kooky, kilted, and tattooed as I want to be.

Thanks Loki!

# FOR LOKI

## by Oliver Leon Porter

O Torchlighter God.
Weave us a web of words
to bring joy and laughter.
Wayfinder, may your torch
lead us to hearth and home.

Son of Farbauti and Laufey,
Son of lightning and leaves,
You make family of misfits
and comrades of trans people.
So too may we have welcoming arms.

Ferocious Flame-hair,
You embody change and cycle
—switching from male to female to—
so may we delight in fabulous shifts.

Husband to Sigyn,
You survive under Her bowl.
May we hold any poison
with great caution,
and be so committed to love.

You are Odin's benchmate:
May our friendships be so firm
and our drinking horn be full
of laughter!

Sacred Shapeshifter,
gender-changer,
joy of our hearts,
bless us with energy
in the long fight
for transgender rights.

Shapeshifter, may the forms
we inhabit be bright like You.

Horsemother, may we ride forth with friends.
Snakefather, may there be no false tongues here.
Deathfather, may there be transformation here.
Wolffather, may we be released from our bonds.

Bless us with inspiration.
Bless us with battle-gladness.
May the games we play honour You.
May our doors ever be open to You, even when others turn You away.
May the trickster god be welcome in our hearts!

Hail Loki!

# LOKI'S POETRY

## by Eleanor Wood

Watch the wild horse run free.
Notch your runes upon the tree.
Drink the potion from a bee.
Blink thrice and you shall see.
Loki's secret poetry.

*Silver mask-shaped ornament (actual length 27 mm) from Slagelse, Zealand, Denmark. A number of mask ornaments like this have been found recently with vertical lines on or across the lips. These may represent Loki with his sewn or scarred mouth. See Pentz, "Viking Art, Snorri Sturlusson and Some Recent Metal Detector Finds." Fornvännen, vol. 113 (2008), pp. 17-33. Image courtesy of the National Museum of Denmark. Photo by Søren Greve, CC BY-SA 4.0.*

*Art by Katrina Kunstmann, digital*

# Comics

47

48

49

50

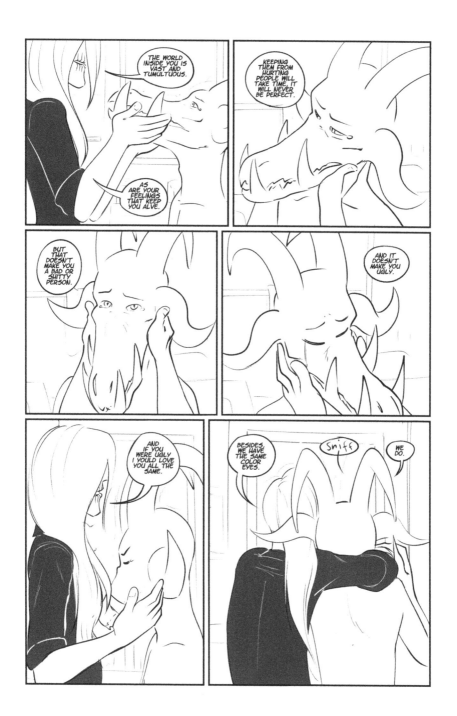

51

53

# Short Stories

# THE WALLS OF ASGARD

## by Luke Babb

You want to know about Sleipnir? Now that's a story worth telling. Come close, wanderer, and sit—we three wot this one well.

Now this was at the very beginning—Midgard new and green with its first coat, Valhalla still spotless and empty, the kegs being rolled in one by one. The gods were very pleased with themselves and had gathered together in a field to drink and consider their next major project.

"I think," Freyr said, pushing up onto one elbow as he spoke. "No, shh, listen. I think the alfs need a place to go."

"Big surprise," Loki muttered, turning his face enough that the words would travel to his companions rather than into the earth. "Wouldn't it technically be yours, if they had one?"

"No, listen," Freyr said, his head falling back as Freyja giggled. "Shh. What are they going to do, just live in the hills? Just—" He collapsed back onto the ground, sticking his hands up and making a little plopping noise as one hand went into the other. "Just like that?"

"Some of them," Odin said, pulling his hat down over his eye. The empty socket was still red and sore-looking, and he was sensitive about it. "Some of them can live in the hills. Some might have their own land, in time."

"Plop," Freyr said, hiding one hand inside the other again as he broke into laughter, dark eyes merry as his sister's. He had met Byggvir and Beyla just the day before, and they were quickly becoming his favorites.

"Where are *we* going to live?" Loki asked. "We can't just—wander around making things forever."

"Why not?" Odin pushed the hat back up and fixed his eye on his brother.

"Because I'm tired and my feet hurt," Loki said, having just made up the idea of feet and finding them very entertaining. "And if the alfs get a place to live, we should too. Hoenir, tell him."

Hoenir looked between his brothers and shrugged. This was back before the wars, but even then, he was a god of few words.

Loki sighed. "Think about it. Ask and Embla are already going at it—

there's not going to be enough room here for all of us much longer. We need to have someplace we can come back to. The Jotnar are already working on something out East."

A tangle of red hair came out of one of the clumps of grass as Thor blinked himself awake. "Not too close to the humans, I hope?"

Loki shrugged. "Close enough? They're calling it Jotunheim. I haven't really had a chance to visit."

Thor stood, rolling his shoulders and cracking his neck. The sound boomed across the valley.

"Must we?" asked Frigga as the rain began to fall. "Right now?" She tucked her spindle under a sleeve to keep the wool dry.

"I'll just go take a look," Thor said.

He set off in a direction that was really mostly very eastward. The rain followed after him, leaving the field only slightly more soggy than it had started.

Loki groaned and stuck his face back into the mud. That was going to be a mess. He'd worry about it after the hangover wore off.

He was like that still, drowsing in the dirt, when the new voice interrupted.

"I can build a fortress for you."

The gods all looked up at the newcomer, standing comfortably at the edge of the valley.

He was a big man, all rocky shoulders and hard hands calloused with long work, with a hammer and a pick hanging off of his belt. Once he saw that he had their attention, he nodded, satisfied. "Three seasons. Best fortress you could ask for. Solid, trustworthy—even if the trolls get to Midgard, they won't be able to touch it."

He looked in the direction that Thor had gone off in, and frowned a little.

Loki and Odin shared a look, measuring each other's reactions. Odin pushed his hat a little further back on his forehead. "That is a bold claim indeed. What would you require for this great service?"

"Her hand in marriage," the newcomer said, nodding to Freyja where she lounged, her head on Freyr's stomach. "And hers," he said, nodding to Sunna. He paused. "And his," he said, gesturing to Mani.

"I beg your pardon?" Sunna asked, sitting up in a blaze of light.

Mani sat up as well, looking at the newcomer much more thoughtfully.

"Greedy," muttered Freyr, his hand pausing as he stroked his sister's head.

"Can you do it in one season?" asked Loki. "Can you do it by next summer?"

The newcomer frowned at him—not angry, but considering his options. "Winter is about to begin. Can I use my horse?" he asked, nodding behind him.

The stallion that stepped out was a paragon of his breed, the ur-stallion. A strong head sat atop a neck like a waterfall, legs like the trunks of trees. Looking at him, Loki knew two things—this man and his steed were jotun, and they *absolutely* needed to build the fortress.

"Done," he said, and the gods all turned to look at him.

Freyja sat up, rage flickering in the back of her eyes. "I did not say—"

"I said done," Loki repeated, feeling entirely sober as he shot Odin another look.

Odin waited for a long moment, watching him.

"All right," he said, eventually, standing to offer the newcomer his hand. "You have my word."

The builder looked to the east again, and then at Mani's shining face. "You'll all witness this?"

"We will," said the gods, and the oath fell into place, woven between them.

Time, in those days, was a malleable thing that flexed and moved as was most appropriate to its story—but the seasons had been set. Winter started and their smith began to work, his pick carving off great boulders from the mountains and his horse carrying three, four, six at a time, back to the meadow, hardly straining as he dragged the sledge behind him.

"That's impossible," Frigga said, looking up from her plans for the kitchen.

"That's obscene," Njordr said, harvesting the first of their crops.

"Isn't it?" Loki asked, watching the builder wipe his brow, watching the horse's withers shake.

The darkest days came and the fortress rose up around them, each stone taller than any one of them as they worked within it, making spaces for each of their gifts.

"How is this possible?" Heimdall asked, watching the builder lay mortar between the stones.

"How are we going to pay him?" Freyr asked, holding his sister's hand in her new hall.

"What's his name?" Loki asked, petting the nose of the builder's horse.

"Svadilfari," said the jotnar, recognizing Loki as a kinsman. "Has Thor returned?"

"Not yet," Loki said, looking to the east.

Winter faded, and the grass grew green again. When three days remained until summer, the fortress was complete, except for the finishing stones that would make the entrance. The gods gathered in their new hall, steps ringing on the even stones beneath them.

"This is nice," Loki said, admiring the craftsmanship. "Isn't this nice? Look at how he set the window, that's—"

"What," Freyja asked, "are we going to do? He is going to make his deadline, that's very clear."

"I mean, we're going to marry him, aren't we?" Mani cast a look around the room, gentle and kind and seemingly not at all bothered by the idea.

"We are not," Sunna said, as if that was the end of the discussion. "He is *definitely* a jotun. I can feel it."

"Uh," said Loki. "So are—I mean, most of us? Most of us have jotun blood. My father was literally a lightning bolt."

"I thought your father was Ymir?" Bragi asked. "Not that it matters, but, for the story—"

"Things were complicated," Loki said. "They overlapped. Not the point. He has our word, he's met our price. We have to pay him."

"And whose fault is that?" Odin asked, eye gleaming in the shadow of his hat.

Loki turned, slowly, to look at his brother. "I'd say it's the fault of the man who shook his hand, myself."

"Weren't you the one to say it was a deal?" Odin asked, voice as dark and as soft as his cloak.

"He was," Heimdall agreed, arms crossing as he watched Loki.

"Sure, but the deal is made." Loki said. "It's an *oath*, we can't just—"

"Maybe we can't," Sunna agreed. "But that doesn't mean I have to go quietly."

Freyja stood up. She had been very quiet, but the look in her eyes was of power awakening: rage and magic building on the tongue. She turned it on Loki.

"I am not pleased to be sold as some—some sort of hostage," she said, and there was a fire to her words like prophecy sometimes carries. "If I must pay for you, then you must pay something to me, Loki."

The world was new, but even then, violence was old, and she carried it in every line of her.

Loki lifted his hands and kept his expression very solemn. "Okay. Okay, I'll fix it. He won't finish the wall, I give you my word."

"Give me your oath," Freyja said, holding her hand out.

"That too," Loki agreed, and they shook on it.

That night, in his quarry, the builder carved the last few stones. They were massive things—the keystone for Asgard's gate and the stone on either side, each as big as the builder himself, and four times as heavy. He heaved them, one by one, onto the sledge he had built. It was long, difficult work that left him panting, but Svadilfari was strong enough to carry the loaded sledge back to Asgard in no time at all. It had been difficult work, but well done—and he was pleased to think of the reward he would earn.

The builder was setting the harness on his stallion's shoulders when the horse's nose flared, white showing around his eyes. He tossed his head, lips pulling back as he snorted, stamping on the ground.

"What's wrong, boy?" asked the builder, looking around. "What—"

He saw the mare on the ridge above them, outlined against the sky. She was too large to be anything but jotun, her lines perfect as she cantered past, tail swishing. The builder tried to grab onto Svadlifari, but it was too late. The stallion bucked free of his hands, broke the traces of the sledge, and raced up the slope towards the space where the mare, breaking into a gallop, disappeared.

The builder looked at the three massive stones. He considered the weight of each one, the long road back to Asgard's half-finished gate. He, too, took off after the mare.

They ran through the night, the mare leading them into woods and fields, until the builder saw the sun rising and knew he could not spare any more time. If he could not count on his horse for help, he would have to carry the stones himself—and it was a long way back to the quarry, with only two days left to build.

He gathered up the first of the stones and carried it back, laying it in place after a day. The second he strained and toiled with, dragging it across the great field to set in place at the end of the night. But the keystone was greater than either, and he had only managed to bring it back to the wall when dawn broke on the third day.

There was no way, he thought, that he could place it properly in the time he had left. He could not prove that the gods had arranged this, but there was no doubt in his mind, as he stomped and strained, his form shifting as the boulders of his muscles and the cliff that was his face showed itself.

"I knew it," said Sunna, waking. "I told you he was a jotun."

"Surely," Njordr said, thinking of the brewer that shared his kingdom, "we are not to be held by oaths to the jotnar?"

Odin took his hat off and looked to the east. "Thor," he said, and the clouds rolled in.

Thor came, hands bloody, knuckles cracking as he strode back into the field. "Who is this?" he asked, and then swung, fist like a hammer as it struck the builder's face.

The jotun stumbled, dropping his hammer, and Thor picked it up.

"Nice," Thor said, and brought it down, smashing in the builder's forehead where he stood.

The jotun stumbled, and staggered, and fell into that place where all the enemies of the gods fall, after they have been declared so.

And that was the end of that, for a time. The body proved no problem, and together the gods set the keystone—though it was never so sturdy as the rest of the hall. They feasted and drank and celebrated their new home, so cleverly won, and nobody thought to ask what had slowed the builder's work in those last few days.

Some time later, Loki arrived again in Asgard, leading beside him a colt unsteady on eight legs. Odin was waiting for him, leaning against the gate with laughter in his eye.

Loki paused, looking at the set of the keystone. "Little crooked, isn't it?"

"It will do," Odin said, bending down to offer his hand to the colt. "Who do we have here?"

"This is Sleipnir," Loki said, and as he looked down on them both his face was terribly, painfully fond. "You don't think that *breaking an oath on a keystone—*"

"I don't," Odin said, standing again to look at his brother. "I do think I need a horse."

Loki laughed. "I thought that too," he agreed, touching Odin's shoulder. "Come, show me what you've done with the place."

So ends the story of Sleipnir. What else would you like to know?

# THRYMSKVIDA

## by Luke Babb

Once upon a time, Thor lost his hammer.

(How it happened isn't important. Don't worry about it. What's one detail in such a large story?)

What's important is this—the sun rose over Asgard, and sometime after that, Thor woke up.

He stretched, and yawned, and reached out as he always did. His hand brushed over the ass of his companion, the leather of his magic belt, the soft furs that covered the bed. And then there was nothing. Which wasn't, he realized through the haze of sleep, how this was supposed to go.

"Loki?" Thor sat up all in a rush of adrenaline, blinking through the sand in his eyes. "Loki!"

His companion made a rude noise, and raised a hand to push the loud noises back into the Thunderer's loud face. "Shhh. Hangover time."

"Where's Mjolnir?" Thor threw the furs off of them, revealing nothing but the pallet and Loki's knobbly ankles, twitching in the sudden cold. "Do you have it?"

Loki considered being offended, but it currently seemed like an awful lot of work. Especially with a hangover right there that deserved immediate attention. "Do I look like I have it?"

"Did you put it somewhere?"

There was a seismic shift in the bed, and when it stabilized Loki cracked an eyelid to see Thor's back like a great brown mountain, cresting over the side of the bedframe.

"Last I saw, you were snuggling it and snoring," Loki said, forcing himself up onto one arm. "You didn't knock it—?"

"No!" Thor sat up, and it wasn't the fury that stopped Loki cold—Thor's face always looked half naked without a little fury. It was the terror cresting in the back of the Thunderer's eyes. "It's gone!"

Loki wet his lips, feeling the smooth scars there, and shook his head, forced himself upright. "It's not. We'll find it."

They did not find it. Not in their bags, not in the space between the bed and the wall, not in the wall itself, which buckled under Thor's fist much slower than it would have under the swing of his hammer. When they were finished with the room, there was nowhere to hide even an indrawn breath—and there was no sign of Mjolnir.

"Someone has stolen it," Thor said, standing in the center of the chaos, breath coming heavy and forced. "Someone—"

Catching his breeches before they hit him in the face tore Vingthor's attention back from the heat in his chest, dousing it before it could grow into a proper storm.

"Get dressed," Loki said. "We're going to Freyja."

"Freyja," Thor repeated, and nodded slowly. "Good idea."

And then he turned and left the room, leaving Loki to hurry after, pulling on clothes as he went.

So it was that the Lady of the Vanir opened the door to see Thor the Hurler, breeches bunched in one hand, hair wild from sleep. "I need to borrow your feather cloak to find Mjolnir."

She looked at Thor, and past him at Loki, his clothes untied and unbuckled, his mouth as grim as his blood brother's, and she did not ask questions.

A quick gesture unbuckled the magic cloak from around her neck and she held it out—past Thor's shoulder.

"Of course. Fly safely."

Loki took the silver fabric from her quickly, with a nod. Freyja inclined her head, and put her hand on Thor's shoulder.

"Come in and put yourself together, my friend," she said. "We will find it."

When Thor looked over his shoulder, Loki was already in the air, and there was no one to argue with.

Loki flew fast and keen-eyed. He had paid for Mjolnir with his own head, with hooked needle and catgut and blood, and he took that connection like a rope around his wrist and pulled himself into Jotunheim, toward where the hammer lay.

But small birds, however they are built, tire quickly, and Loki was winded when he came to the house of Thrym.

He landed, two-footed, and stood to the height his blood afforded him. He stepped into his kinsman's hall a giant among giants—and still it was clear how thoroughly he was outmatched. Alone, he looked at Thrym Giantmaster, at the members of the household, at the great dogs that lay beside the hearth. Alone, Loki stepped in, and was greeted with a smile.

"Hello, cousin!" Thrym said, from the high seat of the hall. "What brings you so far from Asgard? Not bad news, I hope?"

"I have heard better," Loki said, and it was hard enough to stand and speak without gasping for air—he had no energy for banter. "Have you hidden it?"

Thrym's head tilted, and his smile grew wider. "The hammer, you mean? Yes. Yes, I have."

He waited, expectant, as Loki stood silent in the doorway. None of the giants stepped toward them—nobody moved at all.

Thrym frowned. "And you won't be getting it back, unless I am given Freyja as my wife."

It is very rude to leave a house without a word, without accepting their hospitality—but it is better to be rude than dead. Loki turned, sharp and quick in the stillness of the hall, and stepped up again into the air. There was a whir as the cloak moved around him, and then a falcon darted away through the door and into the sky.

There are many possibilities in the world, and many ways to wind our wyrd—but Loki knew of none worse than an army at the walls of Asgard with Thor unarmed. He flew back as quickly as he had flown out, and when he landed in the courtyard, he did not bother to hide how tired he was. A step, and then Loki splayed out on his face, panting, the cloak a great silver puddle spread over him.

It made a very convenient handle for Thor to hoist him to his feet.

"Did you find anything but trouble?" the Thunderer asked, taking him by the shoulders to shake him. "Come on!"

Loki just nodded, clearing his throat. "I—"

"Speak up!" Thor slammed a meaty hand into Loki's back, and something popped. "Before you forget something."

If there hadn't been a very good reason for the concern, Loki might have kept his counsel out of spite, just for that. As it was, he raised a hand for patience and coughed out an answer. "I found trouble. Thrym—you know—" Loki raised his hand higher, gesturing above both of their heads. "He's got it. Wants to trade it for Freyja's hand."

He looked up to see Thor's incredulous look.

"In marriage," Loki added. "Her hand in marriage."

He waited, hands on his knees, for Thor to process that—and had just enough warning from the Thunderer's determined nod to stand up again before Thor dragged him back toward Freyja's house.

Thinking back, Loki had some regrets about Megingjord.

They stopped—or rather, Loki was deposited—in front of a door that was already opening. Freyja was ready for anything, her hair bound back, a sword on one hip and her staff in hand.

"I'm glad to see you back so soon," she said, accepting her cloak as Loki held it out to her. "And in one piece. You have news?"

"Uh," said Loki, stepping quickly to the side to avoid another painful prod in the back from Thor. "I do."

He thought as quickly as he could, but Loki was a planner, and not always quickest on his toes. So he did what seemed simplest, what would be sure to buy him some time—he grinned at her, like the bearer of the finest news imaginable. "Break out the hope chest, Lady—you'll need a veil for your wedding. "

Freyja looked at him. She looked at Thor. And then she threw back her head and bellowed laughter. "Married? To whom?"

"Thrym," Loki said, holding his grin even as the clouds started to pass over Thor's face. "You're going to be queen of the Jotnar! Isn't that nice?"

Freyja nodded, eyes filled with tears. "Oh—hah. Oh, how lucky I am." Her smile never wavered. "How unfortunate that I will have to send my regrets."

Thor huffed. "They have Mjolnir."

The Lady of the Vanir held her smile still, but a little sharper now. "So we will get it back another way."

"How wise you are, Vanadis," Loki said, reaching up to take Thor by the shoulder. "I'm sure another idea will—"

"Why?" Thor asked, crossing his arms and shrugging Loki off. "You'll have to marry someone. You can't just wait for Odr—"

There are many languages in the Nine Worlds, and Loki chose the darkest one, the one that cracks wood and splits rock, to swear in. It didn't matter. It was drowned beneath the rage of Odr's wife.

What followed was not a fight, as such. There are few things, perishingly few, worth drawing blood in Asgard. And it was too quick to count even as a scuffle. Freyja reached out the hand holding her staff, fixed Thor in her gaze, and with a neat movement misplaced him from himself.

Loki looked between her, and the wide-eyed stare that Thor was giving whatever it was he was seeing. And then Loki bowed, deep, out of sheer self preservation. "I am sorry, Vanadis. We will—"

"You will find another way," Freyja said, in a tone that brooked no argument. She turned her back on them both. "It seems you will need help." She tapped her staff, once, on the hard packed dirt of the courtyard.

Thor took a great shuddering breath and rocked back a half step, eyes brightening as he returned to himself. And then, not a moment later, doors around the courtyard began to fly open.

Then came the riot.

It was not, strictly speaking, anything of the kind. But it was a gathering of the Æsir—and one without Odin to cajole and bully and bribe them into being of one mind.

There was a considerable amount of yelling. Someone pounded on the table with a weapon hard enough to upset someone else's food. At some point, both a table and food were provided for the assembly. Time and causality had a habit of getting wrinkled when the Æsir all focused on the same thing.

Loki had a drink, and the first food of his day, and retreated to sit beside Sigyn and watch the proceedings, repeating his story as often as he was asked. No, he knew no way to infiltrate Thrym's home. No, he had not seen where the hammer was being kept. It had seemed lower—he would guess somewhere underground. No, he did not recommend a war with the king of the giants while their defenses were in this state.

He waited until Thor had yelled himself hoarse, and then Loki looked around. He looked to Freyja, who kept her gaze high. There would be no help there. To Tyr—but Tyr had no wish to step back into the high seat, and kept his own counsel. To Baldr—but that son of Odin had never needed to turn his mind to unpleasantness, and did not even notice Loki's gaze.

And then he looked to Heimdall, who knew the future best of anyone but the Norns themselves. And far-seeing Heimdall, his hair as white as his mothers', looked back, and nodded, and stood to get the attention of all those gathered.

"There is a way to solve this," Heimdall said, and every worried eye turned to him. "Listen—" And he fixed his eyes over the crowd, over the roofs of Asgard, over and through anything the rest of them could see.

They listened, each of them, intently. Even then, the future was not so sure that the gods could afford to miss a true telling of it.

Heimdall's voice was as distant as his eyes when he spoke again. "We put—a veil on Thor. Brisingr around his neck, and a dress, and—a hat."

There was a distinct change in the quality of the silence.

"And keys, on his belt," Heimdall said, his eyes slowly returning to the assembly. "To ring, as he walks."

"As befits any fine lady, on her way to be wed," Sigyn said, a hand raised to cover her mouth.

Loki did not dare look at her.

"I—" Thor stuttered. "I cannot—everyone would think—"

The Æsir—the only everyone that mattered—were stock still, trapped between the weight of prophecy and the daunting prospect of finding a dress to fit the son of Jord.

"They will think nothing of the kind!" Loki said, slapping the table. A few seats down, Nanna jumped. "What could be more heroic—what could we be more lucky to have—than a defender who will do what's necessary to keep the giants from the door?" He caught Freyr's eye. "There is no dishonor in defending Asgard, is there?"

"None at all!" Freyr answered, and when he stood there was a mutter of agreement from around the table. "We will be indebted."

"I should say we will!" Loki agreed. "And I will go with you, my friend—for any great lady must have a maidservant. You will not need to go alone."

"Hail!" Freyr said, lifting his horn. "Hail to the doers! Hail the heroes!"

"Hail!" answered the Æsir, happy to be given a clear and familiar script.

Loki sat down amidst the toast, to find Sigyn already leaning in. "As if you'd miss a minute."

"It's a good plan," he muttered back, kissing her cheek.

She smiled. "Such a shame you didn't have a chance to suggest it yourself."

Loki laughed. "What can I say? A blessing on all prophecy."

One toast led to another, which led to a third, and by then it was easy enough for Loki to extract himself and Thor from the proceedings. He did not miss the raised glass Freyr tilted toward him, or Heimdall's smile, however bemused—and when Freyja stood to follow them, Loki found himself in an excellent mood indeed.

"Will you lend us your necklace, Lady?" he asked, once they were away from the table.

She reached out and put a golden hand on his shoulder. "Gladly," she said. "And any other help I can offer." And they shared a smile that told Loki all was well.

"I can take care of myself," he said, and reached over to slam Thor on the back hard enough that it would knock a lesser man unsteady. "But if you would help with the bridal array. . ."

Sigyn stepped up onto Freyja's other side, all curbed laughter and bright eyes. "The Thunderer will have handmaidens enough to make him the perfect bride," she said.

Freyja beamed as she reached out to put an arm around Loki's wife.

Thor looked between the three of them. He was red faced, shoulders drawn in—and then he snorted, and returned their smiles. "How could I worry, in such care?"

Freyja opened her home to them again, and retreated with Sigyn and Thor into the back. Loki did not follow, but stepped instead into another room, for the privacy to sit, and breathe, and change.

When she stepped out again, the handmaiden could hear Sif's voice, mixing with the others in Freyja's private rooms. Delighted, and with no one to see, the handmaiden giggled, picked up her skirts, and hurried to join them.

The room was awash with fabric—more clothing than, she thought, any one Asynja could need. It covered every surface, discarded or measured or used for ideas—and in the midst stood Thor, feet planted wide and warlike, draped in more bright cloth, and strung with gems. His hands were covered with rings, and clean, and his hair was brushed back into neat braids, ready to for pinning up. It was, by any estimation, a rare sight indeed.

With his head held so still by his attendants, Thor was the first to see the handmaiden enter. His eyes slid over her—and then he grunted and forced them back, cheerfully enough.

"I don't know how to move in this," the Thunderer said, spreading his hands. "I'm going to tear something."

"Move however you like," the handmaiden said, "the rules are different, there."

She stepped further into the room, earning a sharp gaze from Freyja, and a lingering one from Sigyn, as they saw her properly. She hummed, inspecting the edges of Thor's dress. "If anyone has questions, they'll ask me." Then, with a laugh, "You just focus on enjoying your wedding."

Thrym Giantmaster, Thrym the King of the Kingless—Thrym did not expect a reply. The Lady of the Vanir had been sought after before, for she was both beautiful and powerful in a way that stirred the Jotnar. But still Freya stayed in Asgard, and the Æsir all the richer for her suitors' attempts. As great as Thrym was, as clever and powerful the ploy he had chosen, he had no reason to expect her to favor his suit.

So there was no small measure of shock when he looked out of his hall, across the hills and valleys below, to see a cloud of dust and smoke approaching. He muttered a word to extend his sight, and saw a chariot, flying so fast across the ground that fire came up from its wheels.

Incredulous did not begin to cover it. Shocked came closer—but while the chariot itself was a blur, Thrym could see, at the helm, Freya herself, wearing the veil of a bride. And oh, Thrym was moved with the joy of a bridegroom.

"Quick!" he cried, tearing his eyes away to turn back to his household. "Quick—I'm to be married, and I would have my bride know this house at its finest! I want a fresh layer of straw! And tell the cook to start butchering the best we have. This is an alliance for the ages, and we will honor it with a feast past all retelling!"

His sister looked up from her ledgers, blinking eyes that were watery from the strain of small words in poor light.

"Well," she said. "Well. We have plenty enough to make Asgard itself jealous. I'll get everything started."

Thrym waved his hands at her. "Do it quickly! She'll be here soon—and then you will not need to worry about such things any longer."

He thought that, as she closed her book, his sister might have looked less than pleased—but surely that was foolish. Who would wish for a better mistress than the Vanadis?

If anyone thought it strange that the chariot, when it arrived, was pulled not by cats but two mean-spirited goats—well, they knew better than to say anything. Thrym, on his wedding day, had no time for petty concerns.

If anyone was surprised when Freyja alighted that she stood so tall—well, how lucky their lord was to find a bride that was almost the height of a proper giantess.

And if anyone thought her a little rude—so silent, so stingy to come without gifts—well, these were strange circumstances. She would be sure to warm up once she got to know them.

"I hope," Thrym said, once they had been seated to the feast, "the trip was not too difficult? I had expected you to bring a retinue."

Freyja's handmaiden, a dark-haired girl with clever eyes, was seated decorously between them. When it became clear her lady was too busy eating to speak, she shook her head. "No, my lord, thank you. We had no difficulty."

Thrym nodded, and struggled to think of something interesting to say. "We did not expect you so soon."

The handmaiden nodded. "We made all haste. My lady was—very eager."

The king of the giants grinned.

"As am I," he said to Freyja, who did not look up from—

"Is that—" he paused, and forced a laugh. "I have never seen a woman eat an entire ox, before!"

"And eight salmon," said his sister. "And all of the ladies' sweets."

The handmaiden smiled. "My mistress has fasted for eight nights. Couldn't eat a thing. Too excited."

Thrym chuckled, and might perhaps have blushed, although it was difficult to see in the firelight. "As I have been."

"It hasn't been eight days since we sent word," his sister pointed out. "It has hardly been two."

The handmaiden blinked. "My lady is a seidkona. She had seen her wedding was to be soon."

Thrym stood, and circled the handmaiden to lean over Freyja on her bench. "As soon as a thought," he said, and lifted her veil.

He saw nothing but the eyes—eyes like a storm, like a scream, like the slam of a massive door. Thrym thought that what filled them must be fury, and it was a warrior's instinct that made him jump back, dropping the veil.

"She hasn't slept!" The maidservant reached out to cover her lady's hand, protectively holding her in place. "Not a wink, my lord. You cannot imagine the trials of waiting for your wedding day."

"Not slept nor shaven, neither," the sister said, almost quiet enough to go unheard—but the maidservant shot her the dirtiest look.

"Well, she'll wait no longer!" Thrym said. "Just a moment, ladies." And he left the three of them as Freyja swallowed down another flagon of mead.

Thrym's sister watched him as he left, waiting until he stepped out into the evening before she turned her attention back to the new lady of the house.

"Have you given any thought to the management of your new household, sister?" she asked, a moment's hesitation making the words stumble on her tongue. "Since our mother's death, I have held the keys, and I would be happy to—"

"My lady is very capable," the maidservant said with a sharp smile, and for the first time Freyja lifted her attention from the table, gravy stains on her veil. "She will not require assistance with this house."

Thrym's sister flushed a deep, angry, red—because there is rudeness and there is callousness, and what was there for an unwed woman but the keeping of her family's property? A property that had become prosperous under her hand, that should be hers as much as it was her brother's—

"Of course," she said, "but the land does love me." She cast her eyes over Freyja, thinking quickly. "And you would do well to have it love you, if you want to rule it."

She let the threat sit in the air, let the imagination run with what a giantess's land could do when pushed by her rage. "What lovely rings you're wearing, lady. I assume they're gifts for your new family?"

Freyja's hand closed, almost reflexively—and then Thrym's voice echoed across the hall.

"See here!" he cried, and every eye turned to him, and to the hammer in his hand. "See Mjolnir, come to hallow the bride!"

A cheer went up around the hall.

Thrym crossed to his bride, all cheer and smiles, and held the hammer over her. Even through the veil, he could see her trembling with excitement.

"Hail Var," he said, looking into the space he was fairly sure hid Freyja's eyes. "And may she bless this marriage."

And he put the hammer into his bride's lap, a promise of all the things to come.

For the first time since she arrived, the bride spoke. Or—no. The noise she made as she wrapped her hands (rough hands, and heavy, a worker's hands) around the haft of the hammer—that was laughter.

She laughed, low and horrible, as she stood. Then she swung the hammer up, and Thrym knew no more.

The handmaiden slipped neatly under the table as Thrym's body fell, a hollow where his forehead had been. His sister screamed. Then she was silenced as well, as Thor, battle-mad, moved forward, hammer singing.

Beneath the table, the handmaiden watched as, too late, the giants scrambled to their feet. She closed her eyes, and took a breath, and found a silence inside her to match the din without.

A certain time passed before the bench was pulled back and Thor, unveiled, peered beneath.

Loki opened one eye and looked back at him, amused. "Are we victorious?"

Mjolnir appeared beside his companion's face, and Thor grinned. "I am restored to my own good humor, but the dress may be a loss."

Loki snorted, and climbed up out of the space that was now entirely too small for him. He cast his eyes over the carnage, and closed them briefly, and then reached over to unfasten Brisingr from Thor's neck.

"I'm sure they'll forgive us," Loki said.

So ends the story of Thrym. What else would you like to know?

# LOKASENNA

## by Luke Babb

*Sigyn is at home when Angrboda comes calling.*

*At the first hint of her, the weight at the edges of their property, Sigyn dries her hands and runs out to give greeting, heart all a rush. It is relief, mostly. The Lady of the Iron Wood has not visited since her tragedy, and Sigyn feared the worst.*

*"She'll come in her time," he had said, the boys in his lap as they shared the hearth. "We have nothing to gain by rushing her."*

*The fact that she is visiting, that she is able to travel at all, is a blessing. Still, Sigyn's steps falter as she sees her friend.*

*To say that the Lady of the Iron Wood looks inhuman would be foolish—they are none of them human. Rather, she looks Jotun—arms elongated, body tall and twisted as a tree. Any resemblance to a human has melted away from the being of woods and mountains that lurks on the edge of their pasture.*

*"Oh, sister," Sigyn says as she reaches out. "I am so—"*

*"Don't," Angrboda says, short. The bezels of her eyes are cold, but she puts one branchlike hand on Sigyn's shoulder. "I need to speak to him."*

*That sparks real fear somewhere in her, for all that she knows Angrboda would never bring them harm. "He is out with the boys."*

*There is a long pause between them.*

*"It is good that he has them for comfort," Angrboda says, each word costing her something. "I will wait, though we cannot wait for long."*

*"What are they doing?" Sigyn asks, as the fear crystalizes and sharpens. "They're moving again, aren't they?"*

*Angrboda sits, the roots of her pulling up to a sort of ease. "They're meeting. Aegir's hall runs gold. We must move first."*

*"We?" Sigyn echoes. "That hall's no place for children."*

*"I am no fool," Angrboda agrees, and nods as she grants the point. "He must move. As always."*

*"Not this time." The sharp thing in Sigyn is a weapon now, and she is not sure where it points. "It has never been this bad. Let the weavers find some other shuttle."*

*Angrboda just watches her, silent with all of the things they both know.*

*After a moment, Sigyn sighs, and the thing inside her melts at its cutting edge. "I'll sit with you."*

*Sigyn sits with him, as he is getting ready to leave. Holds his hand and lets him lean his weight against her, the way Narfi does when he is sad.*

*"I have to go," he says again, as he has done before. "There are cycles to this. I have to—"*

*"I know," she says, and holds him. "We know. I am so proud that you are doing this. The web must be woven."*

*He says nothing for a long time. "I don't blame him for fighting it," Loki eventually offers. "But what he's going to do—"*

*"We will bear as we must," Sigyn says, kissing his temple. "As you do already. As Angrboda does."*

*His breath comes so deep enough against her that for a moment she thinks he is sleeping. "The future must happen."*

*"Wyrd must be woven," Sigyn agrees, giving him all of her surety and strength, willing them into him. "None of us can unravel the web."*

*Loki nods, and straightens his back. "Listen. We're in it, the prophecy. The volva—"*

*She stops his mouth with her hand, gentle against the scars. "I don't care. Whatever it is. We will bear it as we must."*

Many things are golden. Wheat when it's ready for harvest, mead when it's ready to drink, the embers at the center of a fire, light as it pours from an open door. Ægir's hall shone as bright as any of these as he approached, but the sight of it brought Loki no warmth. The last day he had seen his brother had been golden as well, the tawny light of summer just beginning to fade as he played with his children.

He stood in the cold and took a breath, the cold burning his lungs. He would try to make this quick.

The door opened easily for him, and he stepped into a hall already teeming with movement. The tables were packed, piled with food and drink and reaching arms as the spirits helped themselves to platters that never grew less full. Familiar faces glanced up as he entered—and then away, expressions a little stilted, but still filled with cheer.

They'd been coached, then, on what to do when he arrived. That was fine. He would hate to interrupt their celebration.

A horn was pressed into his hand, and Loki turned to look at the cupbearer, surprised.

"A gift from the Lord of the Hall," said the Alf, his breath heavy with the sour smell of hops.

"And thanks to him," Loki answered, taking a drink. When the man pressed bread into his hands, Loki took a bite of that as well, chewed and swallowed deliberately as he accepted the hospitality. "Tell me, where is Thor?"

"In the East." The man did not seem to notice the way he tensed at that, and Loki was careful to keep his expression flat and neutral. "Traveling to the Iron Wood."

"Is he?" Another drink, to buy a pause for his racing mind. There was no time—they were moving already. Travel times, distances—would Angrboda be there to meet him, with her arms made raw and brittle by their grief? Thor was supposed to be here, with the rest. Everything hinged on Thor being here.

Loki looked at the Alf who held the hospitality of the hall. He moved on instinct. "What is your name?"

"Fimafeng," said the Alf with a small bow and a proud smile. "Because I am quick at my master's bidding and good to his guests."

"Will you carry a message for me, Fimafeng?" Loki stepped up and put a hand on the Alf's shoulder, steadying his neck.

"Of course, my lord."

"Tell her that her father misses her."

The mead spilled, and the end of the horn found its home in the alf's eye and hooked up, pushing into his brain. Fimafeng's body hit the floor before his blood began to flow. Silence fell across the hall as Loki bent to pick the horn up again, leaving the body staring up, one eyed.

"I'll need more to drink," Loki said into the quiet. He might have said more, but the roaring would have drowned him out, as the nearest table surged to their feet.

Trying to fight them was trying to fight the sea itself, with too many hands in the wall of bodies that forced him from the hall and left him in the yard, with the door shut behind him.

Loki lay in the mud and took stock, surprised to find himself buffeted and bruised but ultimately unharmed. They'd been coached well, then. His brother had always been the one for long-term plans, but training them all to be so careful, after everything, must have been a real effort.

He had never needed plans, himself, but it occurred to him that having one might be reassuring.

As he lay there, a shadow separated itself from the wall that circled them, separating the hall from the water beyond. He watched as it condensed, defining itself into a body and a familiar face. "Eldir. Good to see you. "

The other jotun chuckled, the sound of metal hitting stone. "A kind lie, Roarer," he said, offering his hand. "But more than your kin have given since they arrived."

Loki took the hand and pulled himself up, clapping Eldir's shoulder. "Staying well out of their way?"

"As much as we can. It is easier, since He's not here." He looked at Loki sideways. "You won't be convinced to do the same?"

Loki just shook his head. "What are they talking about, in there?"

Eldir paused, weighing his words. "War, I'm told. Some sort of prophecy. We've been listening. . . but much of it is omens, and outside of our reach. There's no love for you, my friend."

"No. No, and I'm not bringing any to them." At home, he had been able to hold it all distant, to keep some perspective on the bigger picture. Here, Loki could feel that control slipping. Which was fine. Anger could be useful. "I am here to set them onto defense, for once."

"Like Thrym did?" Eldir gripped his shoulder. "Like Thjazi? Think— this is not a place the gods come to be wise. They are saying—" He shook his head, and stepped so that he was standing between Loki and the door. "It does not matter. They are distracted, now, and you have other children to think of. Let them stay distracted."

*Children,* he said, and the anger flared, and Loki grabbed the other Jotun's arm. "I am not here to fight you, Uncle."

The silence stretched, time passed, and then Eldir let go of Loki's shoulder. "Don't rise to them. That's all."

Loki flashed teeth, white in the cold and dark as he stepped back to the door. "Oh, no. I'm going to make them rise to me."

This time, when he stepped in, the silence came with him. It was satisfying—or close enough to satisfaction as to make no difference.

Loki stepped across the bloodstain that meant Aegir owed him nothing, pleased to be able to leave the brewer out of this. He spread his hands, pulling every eye toward him. "Well! Isn't someone going to give me a drink?"

There was no move, not even from the cupbearers. All the eyes that were not on him, or on the door behind him, were turned toward the high table, and so Loki turned his gaze there as well.

"No? Hardly kind—I've come a long way, and I'm very thirsty." He paused again, waiting, and then ducked his head and smiled, looking around. "Come on. Either offer me a seat or tell me to get out. Your call."

A figure at the high table stood up, hands tight enough on his harp that it shook as well. "We won't set any places for you, Laufeyjarson. You are not welcome here."

Loki did not sigh. It simply wasn't worth the effort. Instead, he looked Bragi up and down, and then shifted his attention further down the table. "Not welcome, Brother? After the oaths we took, with blood and bonds. You're willing to break even those, now?"

It wasn't hate in Odin's face, as it might have been were they younger. Hate would have been easier. The Hanged God looked unspeakably tired and resigned as he looked back at Loki, and then nodded and waved a hand. "Stand up, Vidar. This is a place of peace. We will not change that, today."

"Father—"

"Do not give the Wolf's father more reasons to speak ill of us," Odin snapped.

It felt to Loki like being struck, as sure as any rune.

Vidar stood. In the moment it took, Loki was composed again, ready to step into his old place and put aside all of his thoughts. The time for second guessing had passed when Tyr lost his hand.

Finally someone got him a horn of mead, and Loki lifted it, basking in the fear and attention coming in from every corner. "A toast to the gods, the goddesses, and every glorious spirit in this hall," he said, lowering the horn. "Except you, Bragi," he added, and took a drink.

"Loki," Bragi said, hands still trembling as he sat, "I will give you anything I own if you will only keep the peace."

Whatever Odin's plan was, he was sure it didn't involve starting the fight here, tonight—but Bragi already looked as though he might break his harp across Loki's head. True, it might be entirely by accident, but perhaps this would be easier than he had expected, with the right encouragement. "You can't afford to pay me off, Bragi—the only gold you get in battle is when you piss yourself running away."

"Would—would you like to step outside and say that?" Bragi asked, face turning a bright puce behind his golden beard.

"Into Jotunheim, you mean?" Loki grinned, and watched Bragi change color again in the light. Then he glanced away, dismissive. "If I thought it'd be a worthwhile fight, I'd take you up on it. And if you meant it, we'd already be out there."

Idunn leaned over, and put a hand on her husband's shoulder. "Bragi, he has a right to be here. This isn't the time or the place."

He had liked Idunn, once. "Wise words. I would say you should listen to her, Bragi. . . but she fucked her brother's murderer, so."

The look she shot him was gentle steel. She had never looked more like Sigyn. "We aren't doing this, Loki. He's been drinking, and you won't get me to say a word against you."

"Why not?" Gefjon asked, pushing to her feet. Too straightforward for her own good, as always. He could have kissed her. "We all know why he's here—I say we give the fucker a fight."

"Sweetheart, the only battle scream I've ever heard from you was on your back, and on someone else's dime. What are your rates? I've lost track." He sized her up, ready to move if she did, and nearly jumped when the answer came from right next to him.

"You're a fool if you're looking for a fight there," Odin said. His voice was quiet, but it still rang out across the hall. "She knows as much as I do. More, some days."

"Not really difficult, is it?" There it was—anger enough to drown out the panic, the growing uncertainty. Loki grabbed onto that line of rage and held on tight. "If she's only as good as you are, she'll flip a coin and grant a victory. Seems like a fighting chance."

"Maybe I'm not always just," Odin said—and it sounded in Loki's ears like a pup's yelp, like a baby screaming for her father. "But if we want to speak about absurdity, let's talk about your brood of children, you whorish, rutting cow."

Maybe, later, Loki would be grateful for the blood rush, the heat of rage in his hands and behind his eyes. Now, he simply looked straight ahead at the empty seat before him, and Odin did the same. "You're seidmadr, same as I am, brother dear—and just as much of a faggot when the lights are off. Or was that someone else I'm remembering?"

Frigga leaned over her husband, then, and hissed at them both. "What you've done or haven't done should be *private*. Not—flaunted out in public like this."

"No great fan of the long ago times, eh Frigga?" Loki reached over, across his brother, to trace the line of her jaw. "Would you rather forget what we did, back when Hoenir and I wore other names?"

The fact that she flushed as she drew back filled him with a deep glee. "If my son were here right now—"

"He's not," Loki snapped, pulling his hand back. "I wonder who made sure of that?"

The words changed the quality of the air, flattened the world around them.

"Of course she knows, Loki," Freyja said into the silence, voice shaking with something dark and held tightly in check. "But you're a fool to say it."

"She doesn't know anything as well as I know you, Freyja." He flicked his tongue at her, almost playful. "Or as well as you know. . ." He sat up, and looked around, pretending to count. ". . . Have you fucked everyone here?"

"If you don't shut your damn mouth, we will shut it for you," Freyja snarled at him. "Permanently, this time, and send you home with nothing but grief."

"I already travel with my grief," Loki said, grinning and holding out his arms, as though he could summon it up and show it to her. "The only light in my life, the only consolation—" He paused, and forced a laugh. "I mean, it's the memory of that time that we walked in on Freyr reaming you, and you were so startled you shat yourself. That's just. . . it's really something, when things get hard."

That got Njordr to his feet. "I don't know why you're so hung up on who fucks whom," he said, red-faced and sputtering, "when we all know that you're a freak, who has given birth to monsters. Now, if there's anything that—"

"Monsters," roared Loki, and the other sounds in the hall, the clink of plates and rattle of keys, were slammed into insignificance by the force of his voice.

He took a breath, and steadied himself—when had he stood? "Big words," Loki said, "from a hostage whose best use is as a pisspot."

"Yes, well. I take my pleasure where I may," Njord said, after a moment. "And I got a son, beloved by everyone, out of it. People say he is the best of the gods."

"Well, that seat was recently vacated—but it's a bit soon to mention that, isn't it?" Loki cocked his head surreptitiously towards Frigga. "Very rude of you to bring it up. Besides, isn't he your sister's child?"

Tyr stood, slowly and off-balance. It would be so easy to reach over, to just take a knife and pay him back for his betrayal. . . But no. Loki couldn't be the one to land the first blow.

"Freyr is a good man," Tyr said, "and a friend to all. He has harmed no one—he is the breaker of chains."

"Do you want," Loki asked, his voice cracking as he struggled to keep it light, "do you really want to speak to me of chains and friendship? Or perhaps we should speak about justice, Wolf-friend, and how you lost your hand."

"I did lose my hand," Tyr agreed, low. He was the oldest of them, and even now his voice was measured, almost kind. "And you lost your son, and we are all the lesser. But we will not get them back."

"I—" His breath came short, and his words faltered. They had been children, all three of them, and they were no longer, and there was nothing he could—

Beside him, Odin shifted, and Loki gasped in another breath, remembering his purpose.

"You've lost a great deal, Tyr," he said, halting. "Didn't—didn't I father your son, and never pay you?"

"Loki, he is bound!" Freyr burst out. "Bound and held, and they'll bind you too if you don't be quiet!"

He really was a sweet boy. "Honey, I really want to take you seriously, but you sold your sword for some pussy." Loki leaned down the table, meeting the eyes of the Lord of Alfheim. "Nothing stays bound forever—have you thought about what you'll do, then?"

"My lord," came a voice from below the table, and a small Alf hoisted himself up onto the arm of Freyr's chair. Kind of a cute little thing. "If I was big as you, and half as strong, I would just—" He turned, and grimaced at Loki, punching his own palm emphatically, "smash him and grind him and boil him to mash."

"Sorry, who are you?" Loki asked, trying very hard not to be amused.

"Byggvir!" the Alf croaked proudly, fists on his hips. "I am fast and quick and all the ale here is because of me!"

Loki just looked at Freyr. "Did your straw sprite just challenge me to a fight? I'm not going to dignify that—"

"It wouldn't be the first time you were drunk enough to talk to your beer," Heimdall interjected, voice as even as ever. "Everyone here is too drunk, and running their mouths—why don't you just leave it alone?"

"Because I don't want to end up like you—useless and watching other people live their lives." Loki spat onto the table. "That's what you—"

"What if you didn't have a choice?" Skadi said. Her voice was cold, measured, and it sent ice into his throat. "What if we tied you down?"

He laughed, rolling his eyes at her. "I am my son's father. It would take a lot to tie me down."

"The guts of one of your children might do it," said the Jotun-bride, and he was frozen where he stood, thinking of the boys yesterday in their pasture, leaping up into his arms.

Loki cleared his throat. "You could do that, Skadi. But I would still have killed your father."

Her face twisted as she stood, lifting the bow off of the back of her chair. "That's true, kinslayer. I still owe you for that."

"I thought I had more than paid you back, when you invited me into your bed," he said, glancing briefly at Njord. "Since we're telling all of our secrets."

"Loki!" Sif slid her body between them, and put down a lovely cup. As she began to pour him a new drink, she met his eyes. "Listen. You're right to be angry. These people are not your friends, tonight—but there is nothing bad between you and I."

She was beautiful and kind as ever, and he hated the world as he wound a golden lock of her hair around his finger.

"You really are blameless," he admitted. "And you've always been my favorite, dear." He leaned in, then, whispering in such a way that every ear in the hall would hear it. "That's why we've fucked so often."

She drew back as if slapped, quick enough that the glass shattered and cut her hand. Blood mixed with the mead, and another small form pulled itself onto the table, pointing at the puddle.

"This brings him," the Alf said, in the off-kilter tone of someone who is caught in the web itself, a victim of prophecy. "He was coming, but this brings him sooner. The mountains shake with him, the Thunderer!"

"Thanks for that, shit for brains," Loki muttered.

He stood away from the table, a jangle of eagerness and anxiety. Finally, it was happening. Odin's hand brushed his side as he moved, but there was no time to look. The door was already slamming open.

They stared at each other, and all the spirits between them slunk to the edges of the room.

"Fucker," Thor said, hammer heavy in his hand. "One more word, and I'll kill you."

"Look, everyone. My dearest friend in the world." Loki clapped his hands together, and leaned against a pillar. "The future is already what it is, Thor. We have to live it. I'm told it's best not to make too much of a fuss."

"I will throw you into the east, with the corpses of the other Jotnar," Thor rumbled, "if you don't shut your mouth right now."

"Yes yes, we all know you've gone east," Loki said, feigning indifference as he watched the hammer move. "But there is a lot that happened there you don't tell the gods about, isn't there? Remember that night, in the glove, when I made you forget your own—"

This time he stepped close, and lay the flat of Mjolnir's head against Loki's mouth. "Another word," Thor said quietly, "and I'll be the one to stop your mouth."

They looked at each other—and there was no arguing it, there was no working another way out.

"Big talk," Loki said, quietly. "I plan to live a long time, yet."

"If you miss your daughter so much," Thor said, just as quiet, "I will send you to see her."

It sounded, for a moment, like a blessing. Like a way out.

Then Loki stepped back, and smiled.

"Well, I've said what I've come to say. Not sure I can beat you in a fight anymore, nephew. So." He rubbed his hands together, and looked around. "Thank you for the hospitality, Aegir. You've hosted us too long, I think—but this will be the last time. I hope your next home is less busy."

Then he ran. Behind him, he heard Odin stand, heard the age in his voice. "Catch him."

*When they come, it is to take her sons.*

*They are young still, not yet settled into names. When they remember to keep a seeming, they look like children—small enough for their father to hold them both, old enough to climb and scream with laughter over his limbs as he shifts and changes beneath them.*

*They are young, and filled with wonder, and when she looks out from the house, they have been caught in a cage.*

*She runs out to them. She is kept from them by a Jotun she doesn't know, glacier white and haughty.*

*"Let them go!"*

*"You must be Sigyn," the goddess says, and Sigyn opens her mouth to speak a spell that will boil the air around them.*

*A broad hand falls across her mouth, and she knows without looking that it is Thor.*

*"Don't," he says. "It will not end well."*

*She looks to her sons, to the woman in white. "Where is he?"*

*"We caught him," Skadi says, satisfied. "We're going to him now, if you would like to join us."*

*Thor tenses, and when Sigyn glances at him he looks away.*

*"Is that where you are taking my children?"*

*After they are left, there is nothing that she can do.*

*She can bear anything but the slick horror of her son beneath her hands, the ways the knots they have tied him into pulse when she touches them—her brain skitters away from it, and she cannot force herself to wound him more. He is a net, unmade and scavenged from his own body—but he is alive.*

*She can bear anything but her son's bright eyes as he ate his brother, as she was held to watch. He knew, and he was helpless to stop the unfamiliar hunger of a much older form. He knew, and they had forced that on him, with the act of killing his own blood. He knows, and he lingers by the entrance to the cave, handless and hungry still.*

*She can bear anything but her husband's screams as the venom hits him. Those she can pause—and in the moments before the bowl overflows, when he is enough himself to speak, he tells her that the pain is a gift, of sorts. There are so many reasons to scream—better not to have to choose one. In those moments, he still makes her smile, and she can see it reflect in him a gladness, before the screams start again.*

*She can bear anything. Sometimes Angrboda joins her, and takes a turn— but the Lady of the Ironwood has her kingdom, and her own plans to attend. Sigyn has nothing but this, no other loves but these.*

*She uses the moments when her hands are free to trim the nails from her fingers and toes.*

# THE TRAGIC TALE OF GUNNAR HENDRICKSON

## by Törik Björnulf

Our story takes place in a small, unknown pub in Norway, on a cold winter's night. Gunnar Hendrickson sat alone in a corner, enjoying a pint of local beer. As he sat there drinking the pint, he felt two looming shadows stand before him.

Gunnar looked up and saw two men. One was an older, grey-bearded man, and the other, a disheveled, red-haired man.

"Hello friend! Mind if we join you for a few drinks?" the redheaded man asked.

"We are celebrating today," the older man said, "and you appear to need something a bit stronger."

The older man presented a large, black and blue bottle.

Gunnar was confused as to these men's eagerness to drink with him, but he was curious as to what was in the bottle. He nodded as the two men sat with him.

"My name is Mr. Wode," the gray-haired, bearded man explained, as he opened the bottle and began to pour three small glasses. "And my friend here is Mr. Lock."

"My name is—" Gunnar began to say.

"Tell us, friend," Mr. Lock interrupted, "what is it that you do for a living?"

Gunnar found Mr. Lock's interruption very sudden and paused for a moment before answering. "Well, I was recently released from the armed forces."

Both Mr. Lock and Mr. Wode looked at each other and smiled.

"So, you're a soldier?" Mr. Wode asked, as he passed Gunnar a glass.

"Yes, I was," Gunnar answered, accepting the drink.

"And are you drinking to your joyous return home?" Mr. Lock asked. "Is that why you're celebrating?"

"I'm actually not celebrating," Gunnar said with his head down low. "My friends and I used to drink here, but they're gone now."

Mr. Wode put his hand on Gunnar's shoulder. "Losses can be difficult, friend. Let us drink to their memory!"

All three tilted their heads back as they gulped down the sweet beverage. "What is that?" Gunnar asked.

"This, my friend, is a special mead, created in a cauldron from deep under the sea," Mr. Wode answered.

"Yeah, sure." Gunnar laughed.

"You don't believe my friend here?" Mr. Lock asked.

Gunnar looked at both men in disbelief.

"Let's play a game, then," Mr. Lock began. "Let us each tell you three fantastical claims, and see which of us can convince you they are true."

Gunnar chuckled nervously in response to Mr. Lock's suggestion.

"How about we add a wager to our game!" Mr. Wode poured three more glasses. He then reached up to his face, and removed a glass eye.

"Disgusting, old man," Mr. Lock said. "Why would any of us want your slimy eyeball?"

"This, my dear boy Gunnar, is a mystical eye that sees all men's secrets," Mr. Wode stated. "What do you offer, Mr. Lock?" He sipped back another drink.

Gunnar took a drink as he looked over to see Mr. Lock patting his pockets. He pulled from his pocket a golden, snake-shaped arm ring.

"This was made from the golden hair of a beautiful maiden," he said, "and it allows you to turn yourself into any animal you wish, once a day."

Gunnar, feeling a bit warm from the strong drink, looked at both men, completely baffled by their claims.

"Sure, why not?" He laughed, humoring the two men. "As long as I can have more of this delicious mead."

"Of course!" Mr. Wode said, pouring more glasses. "Mr. Lock, would you do the honors of going first?"

Mr. Lock nodded. "I once shaved a woman's head while she slept. Once her husband learned what I had done, he threatened to kill me until I offered to find a replacement."

"That seems pretty believable," Gunnar said.

"Ha! Point to me, Mr. Wode!" Mr. Lock proclaimed, laughing.

Mr. Wode stroked his beard, thinking for a moment. "I once hanged myself from a tree to learn a secret," he claimed.

"What?!" Gunnar asked, shocked. "C'mon, old man, that one is one even I wouldn't believe."

Mr. Lock laughed. "He's right, Mr. Wode. My turn, then," he said, scratching the stubble on his chin. "I once tied a rope to a goat's chin, and the other end to my testicles. We had a tug-of-war, all for the amusement of a lady."

Mr. Wode laughed. "That's a good one! But seems preposterous."

Gunnar agreed, as he laughed and took another drink.

"My turn," Mr. Wode began. "I once spent three nights with a woman, and drank three vats of mead on the last night."

"Sounds like a great time, Mr. Wode, I'm quite envious," Gunnar said, slightly slurred.

"Ha! It appears we are tied, Mr. Lock," Mr. Wode proclaimed, pouring three more glasses.

"Our new friend, Gunnar, is drunk," Mr. Lock said. "He'd believe I once gave birth to a horse if I told him."

"I could believe that," Gunnar said, drunkenly.

"That's not fair, Mr. Lock, pick a different one," Mr. Wode requested.

"Ha! You wish! Point to me!" Mr. Lock laughed.

Mr. Wode went silent in thought as Gunnar drank another glass. Mr. Wode reached into the pocket of his black and blue coat, and pulled out a reed.

"I can promise this to you, Gunnar," he said. "Take nine steps away from me. If I throw this reed at you, it will hit you, even when I wear a blindfold."

Gunnar, who was very drunk now, laughed at Mr. Wode's claim. "This I have to see." He laughed as he got up.

Gunnar stumbled out the pub into the icy streets as the two men followed him.

"So I just step away and count to nine?" Gunnar slurred.

"Yes, my boy," Mr. Wode's voice purred, as Mr. Lock began to blindfold him.

Gunnar laughed and turned around.

"Take big steps, Gunnar," Mr. Lock said.

Gunnar began to walk forward, counting to nine.

He took eight steps, as Mr. Wode readied to throw the reed.

On the ninth, Gunnar stepped on an unforeseen patch of ice, slipped, and fell forward. He hit his head on a nearby stone, and died.

"Well damn, that's unfortunate," Mr. Wode said, taking off the blindfold. "I was hoping to claim that one."

"Nope, that one's going to my daughter," Mr. Lock said. "Looks like another point for me."

Both men laughed as they begin to part ways.

"Until next time, Mr. Lock," Mr. Wode said.

"Indeed, Mr. Wode, let's play this game again sometime." Mr. Lock laughed as he waved goodbye.

Both men walked in opposite directions, disappearing into the night.

*Illustration by E. Boyd Smith, from Abbie Farwell Brown,* In Days of Giants *(1902)*

# Stage Plays

# THOR GETS HIS HAMMER BACK

## by Bat Collazo

Performance rights must be secured before production. Please contact batcollazo@gmail.com with inquiries or for more information.

Deepest gratitude to my 2019-2020 original cast and crew (Törik, Beth, Terre, Medb, Aaron, Alejandra, Frank, Hallbera, and Erik), and to Fantasia Crystals owners Amy and Mike in Phoenix, AZ, for welcoming our ultra low budget, indie, queer production. Gratitude also to Cara Freyjasdottir's 2019 Trothmoot myth embodiment workshop, and to all attendees, for sparking some ideas.

A modern retelling of *Þrymskviða*.

## CHARACTERS

LOKI, fabulous and fluid.
THOR, large and beardy.
FREYJA, glorious.
THRYM, our moustache-twirling villain.
AEVA-OTR, Thrym's budget-savvy sister.
HEIMDALL, all-seeing and unimpressed.
FREYJA'S CAT 1, a cat.
FREYJA'S CAT 2, also a cat.
OTHER ÆSIR GODS, optional.

# ACT ONE

## Scene One: Thor's Bedroom

*THOR and LOKI are sprawled asleep in bed. FREYJA'S CAT 1 (hereafter CAT 1) unobtrusively does cat things, and will react to the scene as a cat might. THOR begins to wake up and reaches for Mjolnir. It's not within arm's length. He starts awake, sits up, and begins searching, more frantic.*

### THOR

*(panicked)*

Loki?

### LOKI

*(asleep)*

Mmmm?

### THOR

Loki! Where's my hammer?!

### LOKI

Hmm?

### THOR

*(tearing room apart searching)*

My hammer is gone!

*LOKI yawns, stretches, and sleepily gets out of bed.*

**LOKI**

*(lazily annoyed)*

Fucking Norns, Thor, do you really need to have a masculinity crisis just because you bottomed last night? If I recall, your "hammer" enjoyed everything quite a lot.

**THOR**

NO LOKI, NOT THAT HAMMER. MJOLNIR IS GONE. WHERE IS IT, SERPENT'S FATHER? DID YOU STEAL IT?

*THOR approaches LOKI threateningly, without a weapon, but with closed fists and sheer rage.*

**LOKI**

*(shocked awake, draws Isa rune in air)*

Isa!

*THOR freezes.*

**LOKI**

*(moves forward, talks to audience)*

How could I forget. We're in mythology, where metaphors are expressed literally. It's time for. . . .

*(CAT 1 crawls up next to LOKI and holds up a sign that says "LORE LES-SONS WITH LOKI")*

I should first explain: for those of you who only know me from my Hiddle-iscious counterpart—

*(CAT 1 flips to image of Tom Hiddleston as Marvel Loki)*

—and find yourselves alarmed that Thor and I have awoken in bed: Thor and I are not brothers.

*(CAT 1 puts sign down)*

I'm many things, but I'm not Vanir.
Now, where were we? Ah yes. Masculinity.

*(CAT 1 holds up image of extreme, muscle-bound man)*

Some humans in the old days, much like these new days, thought they knew how women fucked.

*(CAT 1 holds up strange medieval sex diagrams)*

And getting fucked like a woman was seen as weak and unmanly. They had a word for a man who got fucked: a grave insult, ergi, argr, ragr.

*(CAT 1 holds up Old Norse grammar explanation sign)*

Anyone not quite "man enough" by arbitrary standards received this slur.

I myself am a prime example of ergi. Male god. . . sometimes. Perfectly comfortable shapeshifting into whatever form suits me at any given moment: a man, a milkmaid, a mare. . . a fly *(shrugs)*. My bed partners are many and varied. I've even given birth.

*(CAT 1 holds up picture of Sleipnir)*

A scandal to masculine sensibilities. A queer god: and queerness, my darlings, is sacred.

But you know how humans are.

*(CAT 1 puts signs away and goes back to doing cat things, LOKI begins heading back to his prior position near the frozen THOR)*

The fact that this story begins with Thor and I in bed suggests Thor, the most manly of gods, is having some doubts. Doubts are one of my favorite gifts to give. But now Thor's phallic symbol has disappeared. Unfortunately, Thor's hammer protects everyone on Asgard and Midgard from total destruction, so it's. . . reasonably important.

Ironic that Thor will only get his masculinity back with help from Loki *(gestures at self)* the most ragr of them all. . . except for maybe Odin. But that old bastard is a story for another time. *(winks)*

All right.

*LOKI returns to his position cowering in front of THOR, and makes Kenaz rune in the air.*

**LOKI**

Kenaz.

*THOR unfreezes.*

**LOKI**

Thor, please! I didn't take your hammer!

**THOR**

*(shaking fist)*

I DON'T BELIEVE YOU! I REMEMBER WHEN YOU STOLE SIF'S HAIR!

**LOKI**

Well, sure. (*THOR makes angry noise and readies fist*) But I didn't lie about that! I admitted to that!

**THOR**

*(hesitates, lowering fist)*

I. . . What did you even do with her hair?

**LOKI**

*(shrugs)*

Maybe I wanted to knit a sweater.

**THOR**

*(blinks at him, mouths "a sweater," then grows angry again)*

DON'T DISTRACT ME! MY HAMMER IS GONE!

**LOKI**

Calm down, take a deep breath.

**THOR**

*(close to tears)*

I miss my hammer so much.

**LOKI**

I know, Thor, I know. Listen. I'll borrow Freyja's falcon cloak, I'll fly to Jotunheim, and I'll find out who our thief is.

**THOR**

*(takes a deep breath, calms down)*

You can shapeshift. Why do you need her cloak?

**LOKI**

*(deadpan)*

Thor. If you recall, I worked VERY HARD last night. I need a rest. (*beat*) Oh, and also, this is foreshadowing. Clearly Freyja is important to this story.

**THOR**

Huh?

**LOKI**

Nothing. I'm lazy, all right? Let's go see Freyja.

## Scene Two: Freyja's Hall

*FREYJA, wearing a large amber necklace, stands with a cat toy playing with FREYJA'S CAT 2 (hereafter CAT 2). CAT 1 enters with LOKI and THOR. CAT 1 affectionately greets FREYJA and CAT 2.*

### LOKI

*(approaching with THOR, nods deferentially)*

Lady Freyja, good morning. Thor awoke without his hammer today. May I borrow your falcon cloak?

### FREYJA

Of course, Loki. I'd loan it to you even if it were made of silver. I'd loan it to you even if it were made of gold.

*CAT 2 fetches the falcon cloak, and brings it to FREYJA, who passes it to LOKI.*

### LOKI

*(to audience)*

This demonstrates how kind and generous Freyja is. It increases the stakes later.

### FREYJA

Loki, focus. Stop talking to the audience.

### LOKI

You can see them too, eh?

### FREYJA

*(sniffs disdainfully)*

I am mistress of the arts of seidr. Of course I can.

**THOR**

*(can't see the audience, has no idea what's happening)*

What's going on?

**LOKI**

Don't worry your pretty little head, Thor. *(boops THOR's nose)* Off I go to the land of the giants.

*LOKI puts on the cloak and flies away to Jotunheim.*

## Scene Three: Thrymheim

*THRYM sits enjoying his villainy while LOKI flies in.*

### THRYM

*(waves)*

Loki! Over here!

### LOKI

*(lands)*

Thrym. You look suspiciously pleased with yourself.

### THRYM

Why are you traveling alone, Loki? What's up with the Æsir?

### LOKI

Bad news for the Æsir, as I suspect you already know. Did you happen to. . .

### THRYM

Steal Thor's hammer?

### LOKI

*(unimpressed)*

. . . yes.

### THRYM

It's hidden eight miles below the land! He'll never get it back unless he gives me what I want!

### LOKI

Which is?

**THRYM**

The beautiful Freyja as my wife!

**LOKI**

*(raises eyebrows)*

Ah. *(nods, even more unimpressed)* No chance you'll settle for gold?

**THRYM**

I have all the wealth I could possibly desire! All I need is the goddess Freyja to warm my bed!

**LOKI**

*(grossed out)*

Well. I'll let them know your terms.

*LOKI turns to leave.*

**THRYM**

I'm curious, Loki. You're Jotun like I am. Why are you the Æsir's errand boy?

**LOKI**

Now, now, Thrym, today I'm an errand falcon. (*beat, more serious*) Let's just say I have a soft spot.

## Scene Four: Asgard

**THOR**

*(calls out while LOKI is still flying)*

Loki! TELL ME EVERYTHING! WHERE'S MY HAMMER?

**LOKI**

Patience, Thor! Let me land first!

**THOR**

NO, TELL ME NOW! BEFORE YOU FORGET!

**LOKI**

Thrym has your hammer. *(lands, out of breath)* He's hidden it. *(beat)* Funny, the names Thrym and Thor both mean "thunder," have you considered this entire incident could be an internal psychodrama with your shadow self?

**THOR**

*(has not considered this and still isn't considering it)*

LOKI! WHAT ELSE? HOW CAN I GET IT BACK?

**LOKI**

Well, his ransom request is Freyja as his wife, but—

**THOR**

Wonderful news! Let's tell Freyja! *(begins to stride purposefully to find FREYJA)*

**LOKI**

Thor. No. Thor, you absolutely cannot—

## THOR

*(bellowing at the top of his lungs)*

FREYJA! FREYJA!!!

## FREYJA

*(enters with CATS beside her, ignoring Thor)*

What news, Loki?

## LOKI

*(hands FREYJA her falcon cloak, which FREYJA gives to CAT 2)*

When he tells you, I want you to know that I don't agree with anything he's about to say—

## THOR

Freyja! Pack your belongings! Thrym will return Mjolnir if you marry him! Let's begin our trip to Jotunheim at once!

## FREYJA

*(deadly)*

What.

## THOR

Hurry, we have no time to waste!

*CATS preventatively begin to back up, hide, arch their backs, etc. LOKI creeps backwards too.*

## FREYJA

*(approaching THOR slowly but with deadly focus)*

How DARE you deign tell me what to do with my body and my life?

**THOR**

*(fearful)*

I—

**FREYJA**

How dare you demand ANYTHING OF ME? I will NEVER be a hostage again.

**THOR**

But—but I need my hammer.

**FREYJA**

DO YOU NEED YOUR LIFE?

*FREYJA is literally gonna just kill THOR with magic in a second if no one steps in. THOR cowers in fear, the CATS continue to watch, high alert and displeased. LOKI debates with himself, then sidles himself between THOR and FREYJA, intervening.*

**LOKI**

One would think so, most sovereign Vanadis, and so he begs your mercy. Freyja, Powerful Sorceress, Thrice-Risen, Chooser of the Slain. . . please, gracious Lady, you're scaring your cats. And me.

**FREYJA**

*(points at both THOR and LOKI, glaring)*

FIND ANOTHER WAY.

## Scene Five: Asgard Meetingplace

*A congregation of gods. At least FREYJA, THOR, LOKI, and HEIMDALL, optional inclusion of OTHER ÆSIR GODS muttering in background.*

### THOR

*(concerned but oblivious, trying to explain)*

Loki, listen, I didn't mean Freyja would have to STAY there. Just. . . pretend! Once I have my hammer. . .

### LOKI

It's in bad taste, Thor, very bad taste. *(turns towards HEIMDALL)* Heimdall, you see much.

### HEIMDALL

I see everything, Loki. *(glares)* Ev-er-y-thing.

### LOKI

Mmhmm, well. What do you suggest we do?

### HEIMDALL

Hmm. *(looks into the distance, evaluating possible futures)* Give Thrym the bride he requests—

### FREYJA

You fucking little—

### HEIMDALL

But have Thor himself be that bride.

### LOKI and FREYJA

*(at once, understanding)*

Oh. Ohhhhh.

*THOR looks increasingly alarmed.*

**HEIMDALL**

Dress him in a bridal gown, place Freyja's necklace around his neck, let keys hang at his side, let a veil cover his face. And as with any wedding, the hammer will bless the new bride.

**FREYJA**

*(smug)*

A wonderful idea.

**LOKI**

Heimdall, you're brilliant. So brilliant no one will ever remember you came up with this plan, they'll all think it was me.

**THOR**

But. . . if I wear a dress, everyone will make fun of me. They'll call me argr.

**LOKI**

Shhhhhh. Shh shh shh. Thor. Thor. (*places hands on Thor's arms*) You've gotta. If you don't get your hammer back, giants will overrun everyone in no time.

**THOR**

But—

**LOKI**

Think of the helpless humans. (*gestures to the audience*) They're so weak. They need you, Thor. (*small voice*) Help us, Thunderer! Help us!

**THOR**

I—I do need my hammer. The humans need me. (*getting emotional about humans, though he can't see the audience*) They're so small and kind and they give me so much beer. I have to save them.

## LOKI

Good man. (*grins for a beat*) And don't worry, my lady, you won't even need to speak. I'll be your handmaiden.

*LOKI begins to untie his hair loose, as CATS bring in a wedding dress and accessories, and a handmaiden dress.*

*LOKI puts on the handmaiden dress, then LOKI, FREYJA, and CATS dress an uncomfortable THOR in the wedding dress. FREYJA removes her amber necklace and places it around THOR's neck.*

*They place the veil on THOR'S head, and a belt with keys around THOR's waist.*

*THOR, LOKI, and CATS exit one way in a procession, FREYJA, grinning, exits the other way.*

# ACT TWO

## Scene One: Thrymheim

*THRYM stands with his sister, AEVA-OTR, hereafter AEVA, looking out over the horizon to see if his new bride is on her way.*

### AEVA

*(worried)*

Brother, this is very unwise. We were happy and stable. The Æsir's reach knows no bounds. Even without the hammer, they could destroy us. And for what? Your lust?

### THRYM

Nonsense, sister. Freyja will soon be mine! *(catches sight of them excitedly)* See, the bridal party approaches!

*The two CATS enter and lead the way, pulling the "chariot" with THOR and LOKI.*

### THRYM

Prepare the wedding feast!

*CATS and AEVA arrange four chairs and the feast table, stacked with cups and "food" while THRYM muses to himself.*

### THRYM

*(straight up villain monologuing)*

I've been rich for so long, but now I'll finally have the one possession I was missing in life: a wife. Sure, my sister does the bare minimum in this house: she cooks and cleans and budgets and slaughters our enemies, all the easy, natural things for a woman. I'm a MAN and do the real work around here *(beat)*: theft. *(nods, proud of himself)* And for all my efforts, I had no sexy goddess to reward me. With sex. Until now. *(evil laughter)*

## Scene Two: The Wedding Feast

*THOR (in wedding gown and veil), LOKI, THRYM, and AEVA all sit along the feast table.*

**THRYM**

Freyja! My delicious future bride! Why do you speak no words to me?

**LOKI**

My lady is very shy, sire. But allow me to assure you how overjoyed she is to be here.

**THRYM**

Ha, very well, handmaiden! Let us all begin the feast.

*LOKI opens her mouth to take a single bite, only to stare in alarm as THOR loudly "eats" and "drinks" everything on the table, Cookie Monster style. THRYM and AEVA stare.*

**AEVA**

*(horrified)*

Our winter supplies! Freyja just ate eight salmon, a whole ox, and all the desserts. She just drank THREE CASKS OF MEAD. How will we keep the household stocked? She'll eat us into poverty!

**THRYM**

*(uneasy)*

I've never seen anyone eat or drink that much.

**LOKI**

*(thinking fast)*

Uhhhhhh, well, you see. . . my lady Freyja was so overcome with lust and anticipation that she fasted for eight nights! Of course she's hungry!

## THRYM

Oh. Well, I suppose that's understandable. Lust and anticipation, you say? (*laughs*) Come here, lusty goddess, let me sample my betrothed! (*lifts veil and leans in for a kiss, then jumps back startled*) Why are Freyja's eyes so filled with hate?! She glares at me like a burning fire!

## LOKI

Uhhhh, well, you see. . . my lady Freyja was so overcome with longing and love's madness that she could not sleep for eight nights! Of course her eyes are strained!

## THRYM

Aha! You will sleep well tonight, dear Freyja.

## AEVA

(*clears throat*)

Lady Freyja, you are known for your wealth. As the lady of this hall, I request that you provide us with a bridal fee to help maintain our household. Share with me your riches and you will earn my love and favor as your new sister.

## THRYM

Not now, sister! Bring in the hammer to sanctify my bride, as is traditional! Set it on her lap to make this marriage fruitful!

*AEVA is annoyed but fetches the hammer, as the CATS move the table out of the way. AEVA lays the hammer on THOR's lap.*

*THOR grips the hammer handle and begins laughing under the veil, first softly then louder and louder. THOR lifts the hammer, rips off the veil, and cackles as he kills both THRYM and AEVA with the hammer. They both die dramatically.*

*THOR poses with his hammer held high.*

**THOR**

YES!

*LOKI hides her face in her hands, then looks up wryly to the audience. LOKI stands, takes off his handmaiden dress, and approaches the audience as if to deliver a final speech.*

**LOKI**

And so, you see—

**THOR**

LOKI! Look! *(stops posing to gesture at the audience with Mjolnir, delighted)* There are humans!

*LOKI looks mildly impressed at THOR.*

**LOKI**

*(dryly)*

I'd no idea.

**THOR**

*(approaching and speaking to audience)*

HUMANS! MY FRIENDS! I have learned a great lesson today! It does not matter what garb I wear *(gestures to dress)* or who I love *(claps hand on LOKI's shoulder and yanks him closer when he says this: LOKI looks surprised and touched by the mention of love, then takes a moment to conceal this as THOR continues speaking)* or how I do so. I am a god! There are no boxes big enough to contain me!

**LOKI**

*(amused, proud)*

Indeed, Thor.

**THOR**

THE BOXES ARE ALL TOO SMALL. Because I'm the BIGGEST of the Æsir. (*flexing*) The STRONGEST ÁS.

*Pronounced "ass". CAT 1 holds up sign describing "Ás, singular noun, Æsir god".*

**THOR**

Right, Loki?

**LOKI**

No doubt about it. (*addresses the audience again*) And that, my dear gentlefolk, is how Thor got his hammer back.

**END**

*Rehearsal in early 2020 in Phoenix, AZ, borrowing Freyja's falcon cloak.
Foreground left to right: Törik Björnulf as Thor, Bat Collazo as Loki,
Beth Rodriguez as Freyja.*

*Rehearsal in early 2020 in Phoenix, AZ, the bride's firey glare.
From left to right: Bat Collazo as Handmaiden Loki, Törik Björnulf as
Bridal "Freyja" Thor, Terre Steed as Thrym, Medb O'Broin as Aeva.*

*Loki bound. Illustration by W. G. Collingwood,*
*from Olive Bray,* The Elder or Poetic Edda *(1908)*

# Rituals

# HOLDING THE BOWL

## by Bat Collazo

*"Hapt sá liggja*  *und hvera lundi*
*lægjarns líki*   *Loka ápekkjan;*
*þar sitr Sigyn*   *þeygi of sínum*
*ver vel glýjuþ:*   *vituþ enn eþa kvat?"*

*"I saw lying bound in Cauldron-grove*
*one like the form  of guile-loving Loki.*
*And there sat Sigyn, yet o'er her husband*
*rejoicing little.   —Would ye know further, and what?"*
—*Völuspá*, stanza 35[62]

## Loki's Binding

*"Then Loki went forth and hid himself in Franang's stream in the form of a salmon, where the gods caught him and bound him with the guts of his son Narfi. But his other son Vali was turned into a wolf. Skadi took a poisonous snake and fastened it up over Loki, so that poison dripped from it upon his face. Sigyn, his wife, sat by, and held a basin under the drops. And when the basin was full she cast the poison away, but meanwhile the drops fell upon Loki, and he struggled so fiercely against it that the whole earth shook with his strivings, which are now called earthquakes."*
(from the prose conclusion of *Lokasenna*)[63]

Loki is and is not a bound god.

Over my years as a Lokean, I've been asked questions about Loki's binding: Why would I want to give power to a god who, when freed from his bindings, will destroy the world? Can Loki even interact with his followers or respond to prayers if he's bound?

---

62. Bray, Oliver, trans. Sigufusson, Saemund. *The Elder or Poetic Edda*. The Viking Club, King's Weighhouse Rooms, London, 1908. p. 288-289.
63. Ibid. p. 269.

These questions—sometimes earnest, sometimes one more way to den-igrate Loki—feel short-sighted to me. The genuine question-askers tend to be the same people who ask how Baldr can be worshipped if he's dead. This viewpoint follows linear time and chronology, which runs counter to my own more cyclical views. This viewpoint also hints at a very literal interpre-tation of Ragnarok, paired with the belief that Ragnarok has yet to happen. Instead, I suggest that it happened, it is happening, it will happen. I hold many truths at once: Loki's binding as a way for early humans to explain earthquakes. Loki's binding as very, very real, with real consequences on a real spiritual plane. Loki's binding as a way to understand the ways we ourselves are chained. Infinite other interpretations.

Time is a human construct, and not all humans see it the same way. Old Norse grammar creates significant modern ambiguity and a "simultaneity of myth": for instance, Loki's declaration of Baldr's death during *Lokasenna* has wording that can be interpreted as responsibility for Baldr's death in the "past," active plans to arrange for Baldr's death in the "present," or the inevitability of arranging Baldr's death in the "future," all at once.[64] The language of the lore itself troubles linear conceptions of time.[65]

This means that, for me, Loki is always both bound and unbound, the ultimate Schrodinger's cat. In scientific terms, this is called "quantum su-perimposition". The pagans I know call it "mythic time".

One of the beautiful things about Heathen gods, I think, is their capac-ity for feeling both joy and suffering, and their capacity for making choic-es—sometimes the wrong choices, depending on one's point of view—based on those feelings. I live in an overculture often filled with ideas about an omniscient, omnipotent, impassive, and perfect god, chased down by a second layer of patriarchal obsession with cold logic and the dismissal of the intuitive, the felt, the irrational. Heathen gods stand in stark contrast. I believe the things these gods experience are genuine, in all the ways that matter. I don't see them as an empty morality play enacted by archetypal puppets. And from the very beginning of my journey into Heathenry, I felt comforted and empowered in my own flawed humanity when I saw it reflected in the divine.

---

64. Lindow, John. *Handbook of Norse Mythology*. ABC-CLIO, 2001. p. 39-43.
65. For further reading, Paul C. Bauschatz' *The Well and the Tree* (1982) also argues that early Germanic understandings of time were unrelated to a modern focus on past-present-future.

I love Loki for limitless reasons, in infinite contexts. One space of many where I can express my devotion is here, in the Cave, the space-time where he is bound. To be human and to be allowed to witness and offer comfort to someone in their worst, most difficult moments is a gift. When this someone is a god, the experience of true reciprocity between human and deity reveals itself.

### Holding the Bowl: A Modern Ritual

We have no known, attested rituals in historical sources that directly reference Loki's binding or spiritual practice around this theme. However, many modern devotees have found ourselves moved by Loki's binding and Sigyn's loyalty, and have constructed our own rituals.

While reading my version of what is commonly known amongst Lokeans as "Holding the Bowl," keep in mind that there is no "historically accurate" way to perform this ritual, and no one true way. If you feel called to form a spiritual practice linked to Loki's binding, I encourage you to experiment and make it your own.

Thank you to Melanie Lokadottir for teaching me about the concept of bowl holding many years ago, though our methods for this ritual are entirely different.

### Intentions

The ritual intentions behind performing a bowl holding can be as diverse as the people who conduct it, or may even vary between sessions. Setting specific intentions beforehand may help guide your experience for a specific spiritual or magical purpose. Alternatively, entering the cave astrally without any specific ideas in mind may open you to experiencing something unexpected, which can sometimes be profound.

For some, the act is specifically a devotion to Sigyn, a way of offering her respite and worship. For me, while I love Sigyn very much, the focus of my own intention tends at most times to center around Loki—Loki's experience and mental or "physical" states, closeness with Loki even in his worst moments, witnessing the capacity for a deity to also suffer, my offering of comfort, a willing duty of love, sacrifice, devotion. Others may focus on Loki's children first and foremost, or perhaps even the snake. Still others experience holding the bowl as an internal journey, a way of calling on Sigyn and Loki to seek the spaces where aspects of yourself have been bound away, or to spend time with your own suffering or trauma.

The act of holding the bowl may take many forms: for some, it is a meditation, visualization, or an internal exploration journey—perhaps a psychological one, or one with some spiritual elements as well. For others, it involves simple physical endurance, and little-to-no mental or "psychic ability" involvement. For others, it involves full-blown astral travel to the Cave.

Though not everyone may identify it as such, I consider holding the bowl to fall under the category of *seidr*, or Old Norse trance magic, due to my experiences here of altered consciousness and journeying.

Though I trance and travel for this ritual, no one else is obligated to do so. The act of holding the bowl alone is a worthwhile practice and offering.

**Ritual Supplies**

- A bowl (I keep a regular brass bowl I use only for this purpose, but when away from home without it, I will use anything available, i.e. a coffee mug, soup bowl, or even my own cupped hands)
- An optional water tap that may be set to drip (I typically use a shower; during one bowl hold out in the mountains, I did not catch actual drips in the physical world)
- A black ribbon (tied around the tap or showerhead to indicate the ritual space, transforming the water in the pipes to a spiritual representation of the snake's poison)
- A candle (lit to begin the ritual, and also to provide an additional source of energy for me while I "travel"—I have held the bowl after the candle burns out, and it is a different and often more exhausting experience for me)
- A dedicated washcloth, and optional other caregiving supplies, like a comb, soap and water, clean drinking water, and even "opium" incense as an energetic representation of pain relief (though in my experience, the latter increased Loki's delirium too)
- Offerings and gifts (some examples of what I have provided over the years: water, mead and other alcohol, rose or love-themed incense, fresh fruit, blood offerings, energy offerings, apple seeds from a previous Idunna ritual, a blanket)
- My spiritual journal and a pen (to record my experiences afterwards)
- A timer (I typically use my phone)

## Ritual Process

On the first of every month (my personal chosen time for this ritual, and not something that may make sense for anyone else), I gather supplies and shut myself in the bathroom, turning off all lights.

I light the candle and tie the black ribbon around the showerhead to establish the space.

I set my timer so that I can be sure to emerge from my trance journey after a certain amount of time. For me, this varies depending on my energy levels and time availability that day. I am committed to holding the bowl *every* first of the month if I am conscious and capable—even if I don't feel like it, and even if it's a mental or physical challenge—which sometimes means a very short bowl hold if I'm exhausted from work or happen to be ill. Other days, when the first of the month falls on a day off work and I'm otherwise well, I will spend more time in this space. Typically, I set the timer for 30 minutes or less. (There's no shame in devotees new to meditation trying an even shorter time at first: 5 minutes, for example.) Longer meditations are often deeper and more vivid for me, but are physically more challenging, sometimes psychologically more difficult, and harder to remember in detail afterwards when I try to write them down.

After setting a timer, I often strip naked for this ritual. For me, this represents my emotional and physical vulnerability and openness. Clothes off, hair unbound from any braids or ties, glasses off, and any non-Loki jewelry removed. This includes removing my Mjollnir necklace I otherwise wear in daily life, even to sleep and shower. For me, this symbolic gesture represents the temporal circumstances of Loki's binding: for the moments when I choose to be in the cave with Loki and Sigyn, devoted in defiance of the Æsir's binding of Loki, Thor's protection may not extend to me. (That said, I don't want to oversimplify Thor's role in this: I have also seen him visit, grieve in his own way, and help.)

I place the bowl under the showerhead on the floor of the shower or tub, and turn the tap on to a drip. At this point, I typically squat down, close my eyes, and allow myself to visualize the Cave, Loki bound, and Sigyn with the bowl.

I ask Sigyn's permission to borrow the bowl from her, to take her place for a period of time.

Presuming she consents and gives me the bowl or allows me to take it from her hands, I begin. I hold the bowl, in both the physical world and in the astral version of the Cave in my mind's eye. For this ritual, I often do what some refer to as "bilocating"—I retain an awareness of my body, my actions, and my physical movements in the physical world, while simultaneously existing in the astral realm of the Cave. More rarely, I will do a more "traditional" trance journey, where my body will be unmoving and unattended while I journey to the Cave.

## Lessons and Experiences

Over the years, I've received lessons from consistently practicing this ritual: everything from learning to hold space instead of rescue, to acknowledging pride as a motivator sometimes instead of selflessness. Sometimes the lessons are about shadow work of my own, as you'll read below. Sometimes the lesson is even that there is no lesson.

Remember that you may see sides of Loki here that are not necessarily pleasant or expected. Some sides of him here reference his abject suffering: screaming, begging for just a little longer before emptying the bowl, begging to die, insults, brutal threats, sleeping, crying, injured, in need of cleaning, numb, dissociated. Many other facets may arise, too, even if unexpected in the context: sensual or sexual, humorous, *comforting* rather than comforted, or even appearing in multiple forms—non-linear appearances where I've experienced the presence of a non-bound Loki standing beside me, even as the bound Loki lies before me.

I can't predict where your ritual experiences will lead you, but I can share a few of my own.

Selected bowl holding moments chosen and expanded from my old journals:

*May 2017*

Catching the poison? In truth, it's impossible to catch every drop, impossible to fully prevent Loki's suffering. I can't ease his pain in full, only alleviate the worst of it. This isn't prevention; this is harm reduction. The drips splash and splatter everywhere, covering my hands, spackling along Loki's bound body, stinging. The candle hisses like a snake when a droplet lands there, too.

The higher I hold the bowl, the less it splashes, but the more difficult it is to keep steady, more painful, muscles trembling.

Sigyn curls against my back, her hair draped over me. I give the bowl back to Sigyn. I clean Loki with a washcloth, filled with tenderness.

*August 2017*

I decide to take Loki away with me, guide his mind somewhere away from the Cave on an astral journey, just for a little while.

I'm arrogant when I'm in love. Earnest, but arrogant too.

I try, without a question in my mind about my abilities, and it feels like trying to topple a skyscraper by pushing it with my arms. With my wrists so small my Kindred sibling calls them chicken bones. A task so impossible I forget what I was trying to do in the first place. Am I trying to push? No, the wall's just holding me up. Solid, immovable, laughable.

In hindsight, I don't know why I thought I could tamper like this with Loki's binding. I laugh at myself, and I settle in instead.

Loki seems amused, sad, deeply fond. There are layers here, spiritual realities and mythological truths, but I get the point, for me: It's not about rescue, it's not about fixing it. It's about sitting with someone's suffering. Being present.

*October 2017*

Poison splashes Sigyn in one eye and blinds her. In this instant, I see her as a foil to Odin: her eye sacrificed for loyalty and devotion, and it gives her rage and wisdom and power. He sacrificed his eye for knowledge, but the knowledge makes him paranoid. The knowledge leads us here.

Later, Sigyn kneels and takes the bowl back from me. She has two eyes now. For a moment, she hesitates. Sweet Lady of Unwavering Fidelity, and imperfect, too: she considers how, as a god, she could trap mortals to take her place in the Cave, until our lives run out, then replace us, infinitely. But she chose this. This is love, even when blank and exhausted, even when dread seeps into her bones. She takes the bowl back.

Love is an action, an effort, not only a feeling.

*November 2017*

I oath myself to Loki, then walk into the cave, in a wedding dress. For the first time, Sigyn allows me to hold the bowl alone, instead of staying with me. It took time to get here, countless moments over and over, moments where in my trances I felt the entire spectrum of emotions: from veins aching to burst with love, to blank apathy, and everything in between. In the moments of apathy, it's easy to question even my own spiritual practice: maybe nothing matters. Maybe I could upend the whole bowl onto Loki, and it would make no difference, here in my mind. Maybe nothing is real. But I hold the bowl steady.

And now, tied to Loki in ways I left only for Death Herself to unravel, and maybe not even then, Sigyn seems satisfied, confident in me, and stumbles away for a while.

I kneel there with my beloved for a while. Loki can't always speak here, but he can right now. He chides me into emptying the bowl this time, before I give it back to Sigyn.

"Giving her the bowl back full is like giving somebody's car back with the gas tank empty," Loki scolds, wry grin. "It's just rude."

*January 2018*

I begin in the Cave, but the space around me changes. Through the gate of my long hair streaking over my face, like the cracks of the closet panels in the film Blue Velvet, I see my lamp-lit childhood living room and the brown corduroy couch at night. Empty. I hold the bowl. Sigyn whispers to me. She tells me that the things I experienced are still with me. I can't be so quick to claim I'm done with them yet. She's right, of course.

When it's time to empty the bowl, Sigyn refuses to let me self-sacrifice. I'd been putting my back in the way of the drip. Today, she insists I have to move aside to empty it, so that the poison drips on Loki.

"I don't want to," I say.

"It's necessary," she says. "Little betrayals," she says, "even in love."

"Loki. . ." I begin to warn, wanting to soothe, apologize, but Sigyn tells me to let him sleep. The less conscious he is when the poison hits, the better.

I'm still new at this, and frantic, so it takes too long. I drop the bowl along the way, and have to pick it back up again. I learn that it's better to be deliberate, to be still, even in the midst of his screaming and pain. I return, and tell Loki I'm sorry.

Sigyn tells me she would have sacrificed herself for him if she could have, but sometimes the poison must fall unchecked, no matter how much she longs to stop it. She taps her wedding ring on the side of the bowl. I think, suddenly, of sound magic.

"How could anyone who ever loved you do this to you?" I ask Loki, thinking of Odin.

"One of life's little mysteries," he says.

*March 2018*

Sigyn is stern now, about my life. She tells me I should only choose to "hold the bowl" for those who need me to and want me to. For those who ask me for it or accept it willingly. And only for those who would do the same for me.

"Give of yourself," she says, "but give wisely."

I begin to see Sigyn as her own force of nature: her subtlety and steadiness not dissimilar to a slow yet unbearable drip of water—or poison.

Or an immovable force: worn down but not dissolved, like a stone smoothed in a river over time, waiting.

*August 2018*

No candle this time. The bonds begin to bleed in the dark, the snake's venom trickling fast from a swollen mouth, pouring instead of dripping.

I try some soothing galdr, singing as Loki screams, giving him a glamour, an illusion, of a lullaby hum and a gentle rain in the place of poison. It works for a moment, remembering a lull in the trauma of my childhood, a dark blue bedroom with rare peace and rain on the awning. I can't take Loki away, but I can bring him something like this.

*September 2018*

Knowing I need to empty the bowl, but the immobility of fear, bargaining with time. Like maybe if I just will it, the bowl will never be full.

I remember being a child with a stomach bug, metal bowl at the foot of the bed, in case I needed to vomit, in the same agonized stillness as nausea approached. A mental exercise, an effort in denial. Like I can will away the inevitable. Like if I just hold still, nothing will overflow.

*May 2019*

Sigyn asks me to perform a funeral for Narfi, for all of them. I do, and my Kindred sibling joins me. I write a prayer.

For Narfi: *You will never be as you were, sweet springtime boy, never come back exactly whole. We were turned insides out, we were changed, but you deserve some rest, darling, you deserve some peace.*

*August 2019*

Sigyn holds poison in her mouth, and spits it in Odin's face.

*September 2019*

I apologize to Sigyn when I hand her the bowl back, and she's harsh with me.

"This is mine," she says. "Don't take this away from me."

It's a struggle but it's her struggle, and she is proud of that, too. It's not for me to cure or take away.

*February 2020*

Sometimes I dread holding the bowl, and do it anyway. This time, I'm eager, descending ready to that space. Like my shoulders get lighter by picking up this burden.

Bowl of poison in my hands, I begin to see it as the Well of Wyrd.

And what a wyrd the Æsir have woven, if Sigyn is the Norn here, and holds this in her hands.

*June 2020*

I see Loki's suffering children, and their images shift and change to the suffering of marginalized children today in our world.

Holding the bowl can sometimes be so contained, so internal, so distant from the human world, but right now, it's about the external too, about systems of oppression. I decide to tell my friends that I believe our upcoming Loki ritual should focus on overt social change.[66]

_____

66. This ritual became the Trothmoot 2020 Loki Blot, also published in this book.

## Conclusion

Not all trance journeys to hold the bowl lend themselves to profound visions and lessons. There is a certain coherency in the trajectory my own journey has taken, even in the entries I did not select for this book, but yours will undoubtedly be different, and mine are sometimes vague, incoherent, or blank. Most important to me is the action—the commitment to being there anyway. Love, loyalty, a gift for a gift.

And Loki, unbound and bound and unbound, has given me the most beautiful gifts.

*Photos of Bat Collazo, during a bowl-holding trance ritual in the snow-covered mountains of Flagstaff, AZ, January 2020. Photographed by Törik Björnulf.*

# TROTHMOOT 2020 LOKI BLOT

## by Luke Babb, Bat Collazo, India Hogan, and Sae Lokason

*The ritual script for the second official Trothmoot Loki Blot since the lifting of the Loki ban, facilitated digitally due to COVID-19 via video conference on Friday, June 19th, 2020. This was the first online Trothmoot.*

### SAE LOKASON

Welcome to Trothmoot's 2020 Loki blot. Because we're expecting a large crowd today, and for the frith of the hall, we're asking that the content of this ritual stay specifically focused on Loki himself. Many of us here love the deities they are oathed or related to. Some do not. We're going to keep it simple.

Before we begin, we want to thank Lisa, Lagaria, and Sonya for the hard work that they put into last year's Loki blot and ve. Everyone who contributed made something that was emotionally impactful for so many people, and for that you have our thanks.

Be aware that there are parts of this blot that will address current events. We will also be briefly touching on some aspects of Loki's story that could be considered graphic.

### LUKE BABB

So what does this year's blot look like? We're doing a slight variation on the Troth standard ritual structure, tonight. We're going to start out by introducing the facilitators—that's us. The four of us will then offer some devotional statements, focusing on Loki as a god of activism and right action. After that we'll have a round of hails for Loki—so if you need to go grab your beverage of choice, this is a good time to do it. Through the wonders of Zoom, we'll call on you and unmute your mic when it's your turn to toast. Finally, the four of us will pour out offerings for the four aspects we're invoking—and we invite you all to do the same. That will close our space.

## INDIA HOGAN

As a reminder, we're going to try to get through all of the people here for that round of toasts. We're only toasting Loki tonight—and, depending on how full this room gets, we might need to do it quickly. We're all Heathens, we know how unlikely it is to give a quick toast—but let's try to be respectful of everyone's time and Zoom's limitations. Please make sure to raise your hand, if you would like to make a toast.

## BAT COLLAZO

You can also offer your toast through the chat function, if you need to or prefer to for any reason.

Please note that we will not be accepting oaths tonight. Any oaths that are made will not be recognized, they will not be acknowledged, and they will not be considered a part of our wyrd.

If you have any questions, or need anything during the ritual, please message Sae through the chat. They're here to help out. A transcript of the presentation portions of the ritual will also be available for accessibility.

## SAE

I'm Sae Lokason and I use they/he pronouns. I'm in Loveland, Colorado. The particular area that I'm in is the land of the Arapaho, Northern Ute, and Sioux nations. Colorado as a whole is also home to the Apache nation, and the Shoshone and Pueblo tribes. The Comanche, Kiowa, and Navajo were also known to have territory that extended into modern day Colorado.

## LUKE

Hey, I'm Luke Babb, I use they/them pronouns. I'm joining us today from Chicago. This has always been a trade and travel hub, but originally it was the home of the Council of the Three Fires—comprised of the Ojibwe, Odawa, and Potawatomi Nations—as well as the Miami, Ho-Chunk, Menominee, Sac, Fox, Kickapoo, and Illinois Nations.

## INDIA

I'm India, she or they pronouns, mix and match freely. I'm in the so-called Philadelphia area, which is in Lenapehóking, the land of the Lenni-Lenape. The Nanticoke nation was also pushed into this area from so-called Maryland and Delaware as a result of English colonization.

## BAT

I'm Bat, and I'll be using ze/zir pronouns today. I speak to you today from the land commonly known as Phoenix, Arizona, land of Indigenous peoples such as Hohokam, O'odham, Akimel O'odham, and Yavapai, among others.

As Heathens who strive to understand the importance of connection and relationship with the land and with other people, we present these land acknowledgments in order to: 1) recognize Indigenous peoples' enduring rights to kinship and stewardship with this land, 2) draw attention to the broken oaths that lead to the popular but false understanding of these lands today, and 3) honor the persistence of Indigenous peoples today.

Grounded here in each of the places we live, we now join together in spirit to call on Loki in many different aspects, to honor Loki, and to ask for Their help as we face the challenges of injustice in our world today.

## LUKE

Lots of people see Loki as a god of fire. I keep my fire in my veins, pumping heat, lending me a goodly hue when I am excited, enraged, in love. For me, he is Lodurr, the god of my blood, the eater of hearts. I feel him in my rage when the blood of marginalized people is spilled unjustly, as they are targeted for premature death by systemic injustice built upon white supremacy, colonization, and other oppressions. I feel him in my passion, the pounding blood that fills my ears when I am called upon to speak out against these systems, to advocate for myself and my loved ones. I see him in the bruises that protestors come home with, the blood raised by rubber bullets and clubs. We are motivated by thought, word, deed—but the energy for action is always in the blood. This is his gift.

## INDIA

In his wager with the dwarves, Loki is able to avoid being killed by sabotaging the creation of Mjollnir, and causing the dwarves to lose their part of the bet. The real etymology for the word "sabotage" is the sound that a sabot—a wooden shoe traditionally worn by peasant workers—makes on floors. The folk etymology, the much more fun one, is the alleged use of these wooden shoes to jam factory machinery.

Loki does not do things the "right" or "normal" way, and normal doesn't work for most of the people who work with him. "Normal" requires compliance, silence, exploitation, and death for anyone who wasn't intended to benefit from it. "Normal" is a widely agreed-upon opinion that can and should be changed.

The teeth of the gears that power the machine regularly bite the hands that feed them. May Loki, sometimes saboteur, sometimes saboteuse, stop its jaws.

## SAE

*Lokasenna* is familiar to many as Loki's disruption of a feast put on by Aegir for the Æsir gods. Nearly everyone is in attendance, with the notable exception of Thor. Loki is initially kicked out of this gathering after killing one of the servants out of jealousy. He's welcomed back, however, due to Odin honoring the blood oath that he has with him. And this is where the entertainment starts, as Loki begins "flyting," which is a kind of poetic exchange of insults. Think of it like an Old Norse rap battle.

During this exchange, Loki points out all kinds of "wrongs" carried out by the gods and goddesses attending the feast. He's insulted, in turn, since that is the way flytings work. Thor eventually shows up and persuades Loki to leave via hammer, as Thor does.

It is really easy to look at *Lokasenna* and see negatives. It is an exchange of insults. But we can look at this in a different way. We can see this kind of confrontation as the exposition of wrongs within our communities and importantly. . . within ourselves. It is important that we acknowledge that we are not perfect, that our gods are not perfect, and don't need to be. We can take opportunities where our imperfections are revealed and turn them into something else, move on from that moment and create change. We can affect our communities by taking the initiative to say something, even if that does mean that we are opening ourselves up to an attack.

Loki is not known for holding his tongue. He is sly, he is cunning and mischievous. He is challenging, and does present the opportunity for misstep if you tend to take things at face value. I honor him when I speak up about the wrongs that I see. I especially honor him when I take responsibility for myself. It is all too easy to forget that for all the trouble Loki may bring to the Æsir, he also provides opportunities and gifts that they otherwise would not have.

## BAT

I call to Loki in his aspect of Bound God, *inn bundi áss*, chained below the earth. This is an aspect I see as inexorably linked to Loki as a parent, too: his own beloved child's guts his bindings, the only way he can hold his son.

This is a god who knows suffering, knows what it's like to be imprisoned, whose pain and rage shakes the earth, and who, I think, grieves and rages for more than himself. I feel some piece of Loki's anger and grief when I think of the reproductive violence against mamas in prison, shackled as they give birth. Or when migrant children are taken from their families at the border—for daring to step foot on what may even be their own ancestral lands—then held in inhumane conditions in concentration camps. Or when Black babies like Tamir Rice and Aiyana Jones are killed by institutionalized white supremacy and state violence.

The anger and grief of anyone marginalized, and anyone who feels it too—anyone who seeks to ease it or even just honor it and hold it for a while, with loyalty, love, and compassion, as Sigyn does? These things can and should shake our world. And even those bound can still fight back, can and do still act: think, for instance, of the recent hunger strike people who are imprisoned organized within the Mesa Verde ICE Detention Center, in a struggle for justice, and to offer support to Black Lives Matter movements.

And no binding lasts forever: no oppression need be perpetual and hopeless. Despite a system of forced stagnation and enforced hopelessness, liberation is as inevitable as change, as inevitable as death: every day, oppressed people break free in all kinds of ways, some small but meaningful, some as a part of monumental upheaval. Loki, Bound God, is poised in one moment of the cycle that endures and ends and begins anew in all things. I call on my beloved god to help all who are marginalized break free.

## SAE

We are now going to begin toasts. I will go first, followed by India, Luke, and Bat. You have the option to either hail Loki using the chat function, or to raise your hand and wait to be called on so that we can unmute you. Either way, please keep it brief so that we can be considerate of each other with our time limit, and remember that we have asked you to only hail Loki at this time. Please also note that no oaths will be acknowledged or accepted during this blot.

I know Loki as my father. He is a "cool dad," that is true. He's held my hand through so much pain in my life. He has been there, unlike others. He has smoothed my hair from my brow—and has put me on my feet when I've fallen. I would not be here but for him. He has challenged me to keep going and live on. I sometimes need to be reminded of this. Especially so when things hurt. Hail my father, my friend, my kin, hail! *(everyone hails)*

## INDIA

Several years ago, I actually ran away from Heathenry altogether because of very stupidly misinterpreting a situation. After I'd packed up or dispatched a lot of my gear, I started getting bothered by a peregrine falcon, constantly perching over me when I sat outside.

It took me about three days to figure out it was probably Loki, two more days to get the confirmation I asked for, and when I put my altars back up, the bird moved somewhere else.

It was the best proof I've ever gotten that Loki was not only as real as something I can't scientifically measure can be, but also gave a damn about what I brought to the table. Since then, he's nudged me into the broader community, making me go against my normal tendency to retreat, avoid, shut people out. I still have to fight this tendency. But in exchange, a huge number of opportunities opened up to me.

Including this one. So thank you, Loki, for somewhat literally taking me under your wing. Hail! (everyone hails)

## LUKE

I call Loki my fulltrui, but that's not the right word. He's my best beloved and first friend, the one I chart my course by and, I hope, the one who will greet me in the clearing at the end of my path. I am grateful for all of the blessings he has given me—but I am more grateful for the hard lessons that have made me who I am. I love him in ways that rob me of words—so I say hail! *(everyone hails)*

## BAT

Loki, heart-eater, ledge-pusher, creator and destroyer, beloved in any shape, any form, lips grimace or grin. Stealer of some and giver of greater. Loki has helped me peel myself open, has shown me myself, as I dig through between walls of muscle and grime and Loki licks heartblood from his fingers. Lodurr, you've given me such glorious gifts. Fully trusted one, Loki, I love you. Hail Loki! *(everyone hails)*

## ATTENDEES

*(Toasting round where all who wish to share their hails to Loki)*

## SAE

Thank you, everyone.

Everything that you had to say here, every hail, every tear, every bit of laughter, was important. It is crucial that we do not lose our voices now, that we do not let anyone sew our lips shut. It is crucial that we continue to speak and to challenge the wrongs that we see. In doing so, we must also be prepared to take responsibility for ourselves and our words. And our words and actions can do more than just "stir the pot". They can uplift the people around us, too. When you're looking to Loki to guide how you interact with your community, remember that a goat and a rope aren't outside the realm of possibility.

## BAT

In suffering, in the bindings and violences imposed on some of us and our loved ones for speaking out, or sometimes just for daring to exist:

May grief be heard and held, may demands for justice shake the world from stagnation, and may all become truly free.

## INDIA

The longing for a return to "normal" is a common refrain now, but it has become clear, even for people who have until now been sheltered, that "normal" is not working. It has not been working. It falls on us now to pay attention to those who have previously fallen outside our consideration—and even the best-intentioned among us need to expand our scopes. This does mean Loki and his people, but it also means everyone else who has been unjustly shoved out of sight, forcibly silenced, constantly and casually dismissed.

It is not coincidence that these people gravitate towards Loki.

## LUKE

Our blood pounds always in us as we move through our days. We are not always called upon to fight, or to raise our voices. There is time for us to bank the fires and rest. This gift does not go away—there is no harm in cooling the blood for a moment as we rest. He is with us in the warmth of the home, the slow growth of connection, the shared conversation that changes someone's mind. Loki is here with us now—and he will be with us as we move forward. But we're about at time, so I'd like to invite you all to join us, as the Troth always says:

## ALL

From the gods, to the earth, to us—from us, to the earth, to the gods. A gift for a gift!

*Picture stone from Tjängvide, Gotland, Sweden.*
*Swedish Historical Museum, CC BY SE 2.5.*

136

# *Essays*

# WHY LOKI?

## by Sae Lokason

I was introduced to Loki by a friend who was writing their Master's thesis on his role within Norse mythology. They had some questions about pagan practices, and in the process of this discussion, I set up an altar and really never took it down. I dove headfirst into wanting to learn about this deity—Loki.

I turned to online sources and was fortunate enough to find people willing to share their resources and experiences with me and others like me. There is a lot to be said for the work that Grumpy Lokean Elder did to compile resources and answer questions for people who came to Loki in the mid-2000s.

Of course, online sources were also saturated by people infatuated with the Marvel character. When I first started out, it was very common to see people arriving at Loki after watching *Thor* or *Avengers*. People find their paths to the gods in a variety of ways, and sometimes that is through pop culture. I am not passing judgment on those who came to Loki via that route. I am also grateful to the people who were willing to wade through the proliferation of misunderstandings about Loki due to the influx of interest generated by Marvel. I can't tell you how many times I saw GLE and others answering the same question regarding Loki not actually being Thor's brother in the lore.

I gained a foothold in the online Lokean community. Sometimes, I look back on the posts that I made and I cringe a little. I had been a pagan for close to a decade by the time I found Loki, and I was still making posts of the bright-eyed newcomer variety. That's all right. We are all new at some point.

Loki entered my life at a time of upheaval. I had recently left my first wife and moved back home. I was struggling with overcoming agoraphobia so that I could try and get a job and support myself again. I was struggling with suicidal ideation, horrible depression, and anxiety. I was struggling with my interpersonal relationships. I was struggling with my gender identity, and feeling as if I would never be able to make any kind of real progress towards transitioning.

Being able to focus on Loki made it easier to deal with many of those things. Learning about the lore and separating it from Marvel's canon was something to do and focus on. Before Loki, I had stalled out in my religious beliefs. Making that first altar for him rekindled them. I actually felt connected to a deity for the first time. I started to cultivate a practice while I was learning about the Norse gods. I started to be interested in magical practices again. All of it was something to churn my wheels on, which helped me crawl out of the hole that poor mental health had dug for me. It was the spark I needed.

Loki was a god who was queer, like me. He was male, but he had feminine attributes and had even given birth. Even though he had been welcomed among the Ás, he didn't quite fit in and was always caught in a loop of "fixing" things, whether or not he had actually been the cause. He did things that were interesting, funny, and memorable within the myths. He was relatable to me, as someone who has often been an outsider.

I related to his pain, too. There were times in my life that I had felt bound, trapped in a situation that I had no hope of escaping. A good many times, the things that bound me were consequences of things that I had done. Sometimes, they were the consequence of how people perceived me. Regardless of where they had come from or what they were made of, my own life setbacks made it incredibly easy to relate to Loki in the cave.

Loki was the one who offered me a reprieve from the dripping venom. He showed me how to break free of the things that bound me to my past. He showed me the value of anger, and what it could accomplish when properly focused and used. And, alternatively, he showed me when it was time to set that anger aside and find the humor in things—when to stop, rest, and heal. He took my hand and offered me reassurance that I was not actually a monster, that I did have a place in the world, that I did not need to end.

Loki brought me to people who have changed my life for the better. He brought me to friends who understand where I am coming from and who have had similar experiences. Once I was healed more, able to stand more on my own feet, he brought me to other deities within the Norse pantheon that I felt an immediate love for and connection with—connections that I was unable to see or imagine when I was in the stinking dark of my own personal cave. In that headspace, it was impossible to imagine that I might love Freyr. It was impossible to imagine reaching out and singing praises to

Freyja. It was impossible to imagine a hail running from my lips for Baldr while I held the horn at Grand Sumbel.

Loki brought me home to Heathenry. He held my hands and helped me heal, then released me to reach out to other gods once I was able to see past my own pain. He continues to be a source of strength for me, a deity that I turn to when the world is dark, when I need to remember to take joy in things. He continues to remind me that all things eventually end. This is especially true of darkness and destruction. It is a necessary part of the cycle, so that new things can grow and thrive.

# LOKI—I'M GAME!

## by Amy Marsh

Before Loki Laufeyjarson made himself known to me, my concept of "shapeshifting" was superficial, like hearing a fairytale or watching a movie where a rabbit becomes a wolf, and then a butterfly, ending up as a handsome prince. I thought of shapeshifting as appearance (or special effects), but never tried to grapple with the deeper implications of how it is that consciousness is embedded in simultaneous wave/particle matter and *the nuanced time/spaces in-between.*

I seldom considered the implications of biological plasticity—growing, aging, disease, mutations—of telemeres lengthening or shortening, of cells growing and dying, my cells completely replaced dozens or hundreds of times, shifting shapes in all kinds of ways yet remaining very much me. As a human, I can barely comprehend this continuous miracle taking place in my own body changing shape (which also contains a multitude of smaller beings), and the bodies of others (many more subtle, much larger, and older than mine).

Yet Loki seems to want me to ponder this. I am not sure why. Once, in a very brief flash, I glimpsed something of "his" own fractal nature. This made me wonder if "he" (she/they/ze) is a being who shapeshifts in more than one dimension at a time. Sometimes I think I sense fragments of this. And when I do, it feels to me like a dance.

And it feels like joy, like a flickering flame.

And not at all abstract.

But most of my time spent with Loki is much less elevated. He (usually a "he") is the focus of my daily devotions, recipient of morning offerings of cinnamon tea. He's the flame of a red pillar candle, the deity who demands donuts on his altar (the gaudier the better).

Loki is the being who came to me in a time of extraordinary distress and deep shame. He ran up all kinds of absurd signal flags to get my attention, and because I was ready to grasp at any lifeline, I gave myself up to the unfamiliar conviction that I was actually in the grip of something, *someone*, quite extraordinary. Even though I oathed myself to Loki quickly, sometimes I still doubt—can this really be true? I constantly challenge my abilty to discern, but I've had too many coincidences and odd incidents to let doubt negate the overall experience.

There's that matter of the electric candle on Loki's altar, for one thing. It has a battery that was only supposed to last for ten hours, max. But this electric candle has been lit almost continuously using the original battery, for several months now. Sometimes it dims or "goes out" but with a "hail Loki" and a shake, the light revives.

Of course, a deity often known as "Worldbreaker" should be able to keep a AA battery going for as long as he wants, but the fact that he bothers to make this trivial miracle happen feels like a wink, like Loki's way of goofing with me. I've only got a tiny human mind after all, and when faced with the vastness of all that he is, of course I find solace in a small thing that I can't explain. There have been other incidents too.

My interactions with Loki are multi-faceted. Our relationship is complex. He is many things to me: beloved, protector, teacher, future psychopomp (I hope), muse, "mother of witches," and more. He ignites unholy glee and sparks my curiosity. I am not sure what I am to him, except that I (like so many others) seem to be dear to him.

And I feel he likes my intellect, passion, and gumption. A self-starter, I'm not a devotee who often needs a kick in the butt, though I do sometimes need to be lifted from depression. At those times, he has shown up for me with tenderness as well as mild mischief and an occasional rebuke.

Though he is not the only deity and spirit being that I engage with (and not the first either), he is the foremost. He's willing to be up close and personal, to interact with his human friends and devotees in all kinds of ways, and gradually (if we're game) I feel he'll open up profound opportunities for transcendence and transformation—teaching us "shapeshifting" of a whole different order.

I'm game. I love and trust him. I'm willing to go the distance. Hail Loki!

# REMEMBER

## by Fly Amanita

I first met Loki in a meadow.

When I was four and five years old, my parents' house backed up to a wide, undeveloped field. The backyard had been made into a paradise of swing set, garden, sand box, and a wooden playhouse my grandfather had built with his hands.

But the best part of my little world was that just beyond the chain-link gate across the driveway lay the wild land I called 'my prairie.' My mother could watch me from the kitchen window as I played in the riot of black-eyed Susans, Indian paintbrushes, bee balm, and buttercups. And as I smooshed barefoot in the mud, brewed herbal "medicine" stews, crafted stone tools with limestone chips, and chatted with the myriad wild spirits of beetles and grasses, fairies and flowers, I felt, too, an invisible someone else watching.

The unseen-yet-known stranger became something of a joker, a playful voice inside my head. He might sing a silly song or tell tall tales. Sometimes he would tease me for being very short. Much too short. Irritated in the way of little girls who know absolutely everything, I would climb up onto a jutting bit of limestone and puff out my chest to prove I wasn't short at all, and he was wrong. My 'imaginary friend' would nod gravely, admit his error, and then mischief would glint in his eyes, and he would say, "but you're not as tall as me!" And he would grow taller than a post oak and dance on the air just above my head as I raced around the field grasping for his heels.

Day after long, summer day, as I danced in the wildflowers and sang to Sister Sun, my unseen friend sang with me. At night, I had to come inside the gate, and I would swing and sing to the stars and Brother Moon and the nice, green lady who lived in the wild mulberry tree that arced above my playhouse. Loki would whisper stories to me then, about a giant caterpillar come to chew the world to bits and a big warrior who had an electric hammer who could fight the greedy caterpillar. He whispered about long-ago witches who had such power in their voices that their songs could force evil spirits off a battlefield.

I would go out early in the cool of the morning, and my friend would show me how to drink from the stems of the honeysuckle flowers and pluck the wild mulberries. In the heat of the afternoon, we would hide under the honeysuckle vines. One day, in the shade of the mulberry, he told me about an evil ghost who was born longer ago than I could imagine. A ghost who loved only gold. He told me how that hungry ghost wanted to murder the whole, wide world to make straight, dead, lines out of the perfect, crooked, riotous, living Earth—the Earth, who was his great-granddaughter, he said. Loki told me that the ghost was greed incarnate, and that she was obsessed with taming and controlling all things.

To stop the greed-ghost, even for a little while, you had to eat her heart, Loki said.

"After that, things could get strange." He laughed but didn't explain.

In the autumn, the servants of the greed-ghost came and mowed the prairie. I wept upon the soil as the land lay there, a shamed, shorn woman. The next day, colorful plastic flags and spray-painted lines popped up across the stubble. My small spirit friends who lived in the grass told me that bad machines would follow the flags, and so I ran around the field, tearing them out, until my father carried me inside, kicking and screaming. Not long after, the developers bulldozed the meadow that I had so loved. They ripped out every mouse hole and rabbit burrow. Crushed every last flower. Made uniform, straight lines. Plopped down row upon row of identical houses on identical, straight streets. Planted a hundred identical, staked saplings, forced to grow in identical, straight lines.

The greed-ghost had won. I knew it. And I knew that I was, after all, short. Much too short to stop a greed-ghost. Much too small to eat her evil heart.

I knelt at the back window, hands clasped, and cried the bitterest tears. Loki came to me then, fully as Himself. Not as a maybe-imaginary friend, or as a joker, or as an unseen presence standing off to one side, just beyond my peripheral vision. He came, not as a playmate who told stories about landspirits or greed-ghosts. But as a God.

He made himself small enough that I was not afraid, and he knelt beside me, an arm around my shaking shoulders, as a father sharing the grief of his child. He spoke to me then in images. The straight lines of our suburban neighborhood. The wild lines of the meadow. The insensate, disgusting feeling of concrete and plastic. The living vibration of limestone fresh from the soil.

*Remember, my little witch, the balance between order and disorder. You are a human, and it's natural that you like the order and safety of the world inside your fence, your home. You like your backyard to be tame and orderly, and that is good. But you, little völva, you love the wild meadow. The tangle of chaos in the grasses. The possibilities outside the gate, the possibilities of utgard. You love all the little spirit friends you have made. When you are finally tall, and all this is far away, remember how this murder made you feel.*

*You have a long way to go, but you must remember, little völva.*
*Remember.*

I did, indeed grow taller, and I did wander far into the possibilities of the utgard beyond my childhood home, exploring other countries, other consciousnesses, other soils, other identities. But the memory of the slaughter of my prairie was never too far away. I never forgot. Neither did I forget all the little spirit friends of the wild meadow, nor did I forget the teasing, storytelling, unseen friend I'd had when I was very short. And sometimes when I read now, I recognize some of his stories.

I see Jötunn and Jörmungandr and Thor in his stories about caterpillars devouring the world. And stopping an ancient greed-ghost by eating her heart? I see that in *Hyndluljóð* 41, when Loki ate the heart burned by linden-wood fire and became pregnant. *Of course, he did.* And all the witches of the world were born.

I wonder whether the witches were meant to help battle the greed-ghost. Meant to help keep balance between those humans who love only order and rationality and control, and Life's need for a wild, irrational, chaotic, natural Earth.

Jörð, the Earth, is the life-giver of the Middle World. Her constant alchemy of death to soil, soil to seed, seed to food, in endless cycles, makes human, animal, and plant life possible. She is the source of most, if not all, Midgardian magic. She is the locus for the landwights and prairie spirits, forest life and little people of stream, rock, and moss. She is the mother of Thor. She is our source.

An aside: I read in *Gylfaginning* 10 that Narfi is the father of Night, and that Night is the mother of Earth. If Narfi is the son of Loki and Sigyn, then the Earth is the great-granddaughter of Loki. Maybe my "imaginary" childhood friend wasn't just telling tales.

I realize, by the way, that also makes Thor the great, great, grandson of Loki, as well as his nephew.

*This doesn't get complicated at all.*

Over a quarter century ago, teetering somewhere between adolescence and adulthood, I took a heroic dose of magic mushrooms.

During the trip, I accidentally ingested a few other substances, went into atrial fibrillation, and almost died on the floor of a cold, running shower. After my heart's normal rhythm was restored and I crawled to a safe bed, my consciousness became one with the Earth herself, one with Loki's great granddaughter, Jörð. I became the conscious Earth. I could feel every person as an individual, distinct, living being. Feel their desires. Their suffering. Their joy. Feel the blood in their warm veins. I could feel the constriction of concrete smeared across my own flesh. Feel the nausea of poisoned land and waterways. The nakedness of once-forests. The intense love. The intense love that Jörð has for the beings that live with her and because of her. And I could feel the sadness. The betrayal of a goddess who has given everything and been told that is not enough by generations of imperialism, colonialism, and capitalism. I felt an overwhelming sense, too, that there were powerful beings who loved the Earth as much as the Earth loved her people. I felt the Gods' terrifying, deep desire to protect Jörð.

By any means necessary.

During that and later visions, I saw Thor, protector of Midgard, and his uncle-ancestor, Loki, chief instigator, traveling the length and breadth of Midgard as the best of friends. I saw Odin and Loki as brothers. Sometimes seeming to be at odds. Usually working in concert. Always loving one another.

I saw the way that chaos comes. How disaster rolls across Midgard, a natural, irresistible force, a tidal wave that leaves human beings, plants, animals, and friendly wights alike standing bereft in the rubble of what their lives used to be. I saw Thor try to protect his mother, Jörð, and her human, animal, plant, and spirit friends. I saw human misery in a trillion forms—death, poverty, disease, anger, fear, loneliness, distorted desire. And I saw Loki guiding people toward the opportunities that are always churned up by chaos, the new paths opened by a horrific situation. I followed Odin down a long dirt path as he guided those who would hear him toward the wisdom that can be born from suffering. Watched him teach souls to how to hang from the tree in utter agony and pass through the ordeal born anew.

I saw Loki again last, in a constellation of images of trouble incited, hubris attacked, and intricate threads unraveled. And I awoke with the total conviction that whatever mischief he midwifes is out of love. It is as a teacher tests his students. Loki may seem to come into your life and wreck your castle, but if he does, it was always built of cards on shifting sands; if you are honest with yourself, generous, resourceful, and humble, there will be no wake of destruction.

Now, my hair has begun to streak with gray. Through the years, suffering has come. Chaos has come. I have done my best to let go of hubris, to look for possibilities in apparent disasters, and to develop wisdom from suffering. To walk in the forests and meadows and love them for their wildness. To love the balance of order and disorder. To never forget.

The God I have known as Loki was always love. Powerful, overwhelming, irrational, fierce, love. Loki, I understand to be the natural, chaotic, creativity of a meadow or a forest. Enemy of the prideful and greedy and self-deluding. Mischief, maybe. Trouble, yes. Uncontrollable and unpredictable, definitely. But Loki represents for me love, in its most warm-blooded, urgent, primal form.

The world is random. We, humans, cannot control it. Disaster comes. Disease comes. Unfriendly wights attack. It's not our place to try to control every variable. It's our place to learn to look for opportunity, to look for wisdom, to be at peace with our own lack of control, to let go of our greed and our pride, and be honest with ourselves.

Greed is worth talking about for a moment. So are pride and honesty. Loki isn't greedy in the lore, and he isn't bound to ego. He is the reason Asgard's walls are built for free, the reason Odin has Sleipnir, Draupnir, and Gungnir, the reason Sif's hair is made of gold, the reason Thor has his hammer, and the reason Frey has his boar and ship. Loki keeps none of the treasures he helps to create for himself. Snorri attributes most of the Gods' troubles to Loki's mischief, but the opportunity to gain from these disturbances also belongs to him, and he is generous with those gains. Additionally, in helping Thor retrieve his hammer from Thrym, Loki evidences no hesitation whatsoever either about cross-dressing or about accompanying Thor into danger. He's focused on the defense of Asgard and will use whatever deception is necessary to restore Mjollnir to Thor, regardless of whether it might be embarrassing.

In short, Loki isn't interested in either greed or pride. And although I think *Lokasenna* has been heavily altered by Christian authors, perhaps the reason Loki was so aggressive in the poem was because he was attacking hypocrisy. While Loki has no problem with lies and deception per se, these are tactics he employs to serve an end, not exercises in self-delusion. Loki of the lore seems to be resoundingly against greed, ego-driven pride, and deluded self-righteousness.

And, at this particular moment in human history, much of the globe is held in thrall to a system that is based on greed, praises excessive pride, and bathes in hypocrisy. Our system feeds the delusional human lust for control. For straight lines. And our system is killing the living Earth. We are killing Thor's mother. We are killing Loki's granddaughter.

And I don't believe for a moment the Gods will let us finish the job.

The Gods will not let our zombie allegiance to a system that serves only death go on unchecked. They will not let industrial, materialist culture murder Jörð the way the greed-ghost's servants murdered the meadow behind my house when I was five.

Humanity, by and large, is trapped in a system that exists to serve the greed-ghost. Almost everything we do contributes to the murder of meadows and the annihilation of forests, the poisoning of the air and boiling of the oceans. The system is artificial and unstable—a tower of bricks stacked end-on-end, reaching to the sky. Any breeze, it seems, could smash the whole structure at any time.

Loki is the God who will topple those bricks—with glee—ultimately showing us all the possibilities we had never seen. Showing us a million new ways to live. Ways to love.

Ultimately pointing us to the paths of wisdom, which lead to a well at the root of the World Tree.

Let's follow those paths. Back to the beginning.

And I think there, surrounding the well of wisdom, will be a wide meadow, clothed in the riches of bluebonnets and bee balm, black-eyed Susans and Indian paintbrushes, buttercups and wild violets. And a God made of love and mischief, giggling with delight.

*You made it, little völva. You made it, my little witches.*
*You didn't forget.*

# LOKI: THOUGHTS ON THE NATURE OF THE GOD, A QUEER READING

## by Lar Melbye Romsdal

*Submitted as part of the Masters in Heritage Conservation program, 2018, of the University of Auckland. This piece of research is dedicated to all of my family who have believed in me, and brought me strength to be myself, and to understand my heritage and identity.*

## Introduction

Today, we have a 21st century awareness of diversity in expression pertaining to a person's gender, sexuality, and place in the world. Yet we sometimes forget that these markers of human identity have always existed throughout our shared cultural past, and are articulated in various ways within ancient stories and mythologies. In this thesis, I will consider the way that gender identity and sexuality are evoked in Norse mythology, focusing on the figure of Loki. Loki, or sometimes Lodur[67], commonly known as a trickster[68] god, stirs the imagination as a chaotic force disrupting order, all the while having a mischievous and free-spirited nature. This god is pivotal in the pantheon of Norse mythology and religion, and is attested across several sources, most notably the *Elder (Poetic) Edda*, and under *Gylfaginning*, in which their[69] place in the pantheon is mentioned, and through their actions at Ragnarok in the Twilight of the Gods.

The sexuality and gender identity of Loki has not previously been surveyed. The starting point of this research comprises a close reading of Georges Dumézil's system of understanding myth, followed by an analysis of Jerold C. Frakes's attempt to explain the position of Loki in Norse mythology and religion. These scholars' works are seminal to understanding the god Loki, and will guide my comparative study of the nature of Loki amongst the other gods and in other cultures. I will then draw on their theories to offer my own interpretation of Loki's position in the pantheon.

Following this, I will discuss the sexuality and gender identity of Loki and how this reflects the social milieu of Viking Age Norse society. I will argue that Loki is more than a trickster god[70], and can best be understood in the context of the mythical world in which they lived, alongside great warriors, kings, and monsters. My central thesis statement is therefore two-fold: first, to fully grasp the role of Loki in Norse mythology we must look at them through the lens of the Norse worldview; second, an awareness of Loki's place in the pantheon gives us insights into Norse understandings of gender identity and sexuality.

I will conduct my research through a stance of "methodological agnosticism," which recognises that a researcher can never escape inherent bias[71], regardless of the disciplinary framework they may employ. In this acknowledgement of bias, the researcher becomes the fieldwork instrument, and in doing so, as Jeanne Favre-Saada[72] demonstrates, suspends their disbelief to take part in and engage with discourse and function. They therefore come to understand something "other" as something known. Appropriately, before I continue, I would like to acknowledge and show my respect to the beliefs and heritage of the ancient Egyptians and ancient Greeks, whom I mention in this dissertation. Without the contributions of these cultures, my research would not have been as complete.

I also acknowledge that this study focuses on a Western society, using Western techniques and conceptions, within a Western understanding of gender fluidity and queerness in relation to both gender identity and sexuality. I define "gender identity" as a self-determined description of what gender (or non-gender) a person may understand themselves to be. I define "sexuality" in this context as the sexual characteristics and sexual identity of an individual. I will also be using the term non-binary; for some, this term evokes a sense of being genderless or neutral in terms of gender. In terms of my own personal experience, I draw upon the masculine and feminine sides of my being to express myself day-to-day, without the need for a fixed and unchanging gender identity of either male or female. This relates to the term gender fluidity, which refers to the understanding of gender as a spectrum which can change depending on the individual's needs.

---

70. Davidson, Hilda E. *Myths and Symbols of Pagan Europe: Early Scandinavian and Celtic Religions*. Bell and Bain Ltd., 1987. p. 1.

71. Bullivant, Stephen & Lee, Lois. *A Dictionary of Atheism*. Oxford University Press, 2016.

72  Favre-Saada, Jeanne. "Deadly Words: Witchcraft in the Bocage". *Editions de la Maison des Sciences del Homme*. Maison des Sciences del Homme, 1981.

In this thesis, I will be using the mythology of Loki to argue that prior to the arrival of Christianity, some Norse people may have understood gender identity and sexuality in a queer or fluid way, similar to some of our present-day Western understandings. In the pre-Christian era, Norse ideas of gender and sexuality may have been a bit queer. It's only during the Christian era that strict binaries were imposed. Loki shows us a glimpse of gender queerness in the pre-Christian Norse worldview.

I acknowledge that the ancient Norse concepts of gender and sexuality will not be identical to contemporary concepts, nor will they have been articulated using the language and ideas we use today. To ignore this runs the risk of anachronism, applying modern-day concepts onto ancient texts. Rather, I will argue that Loki is queer in that they do not conform to stable gender categories of "male" and "female," and thus Loki subverts tradition-al gender binaries reinforced during the Christian era. Their queerness in the Norse pantheon may offer us a glimpse of pre-Christian Norse under-standings of gender as something inherently non-binary and fluid. I am not claiming that Loki is queer in the modern-day sense (of having same-sex desires, say, or identifying as transgender); rather, I am using the term "queer" in relation to Loki in order to capture the way that this Norse god evokes the complex understandings of sexuality and gender dominant in their own cultural and historical location.

This research therefore explores a historical narrative of gender identities and sexualities among a society through its mythology. Essentially, I will argue that the acceptance of Loki by the main group of gods (the Æsir) and by the amalgamated secondary group of gods (the Vanir) demonstrates that queerness had a religious and social meaning in Norse society. I will use a multi-disciplinary approach to the study of religion, with a foundation in heritage, alongside archaeology, literature, history, mythology, and folklore studies. Linking these disciplinary approaches together, I offer a holistic study of the Norse culture.

I begin my research with an examination of the pre-Christian era, fol-lowing into the period of Christian conversion. Poignantly, we time-travel from the Viking Age of 750-1050 CE to the later Medieval periods of Snorri Sturluson in the 13th century. This unity of focus and time (750-1290 CE) will allow me to understand how this past society both lived and defined its belief systems, including how gender and sexuality were articulated in these systems.

This is not a straightforward comparative study of different cultural understandings of gender or sexuality, nor is it denying that these phenomena (gender, gender fluidity, queerness, and sexuality) may have existed within other non-Western cultures during this time period. This research sheds light on a pre-defined Western and pre-Christian society, commenting on the experiences and understandings of a past people, which in turn may still have resonances with cultural understandings of gender identity and sexuality today. I seek to recover the lost understandings and acceptance of gender identities and sexualities amongst the Norse, considering their ongoing relevance.

This dissertation will therefore address these two questions:

1) What is the pivotal role of Loki in Norse mythology and religion? This will be based on a reinterpretation of the Dumézil and Frakes models of mythology.
2) How does Loki's role in Norse religion shed light on understandings of gender and sexuality in the Viking era?

In order to answer these questions, I will look into the conceptual modelling of the Norse pantheon as a system, and will perform a close reading of Dumézil and Frakes. Dumézil's texts, *Mitra-Varuna, Jupiter, Mars & Quirinus*, and *Gods of the Ancient Northmen* are classics in comparative mythology, which consider the Germanic North and Indo-European antecedents of Norse mythology. Frakes's work, "Loki's Mythological Function in the Tripartite System" (Lokasenna), will provide a secondary conceptual analysis of the tripartite system that Dumézil creates.

After this overview, I will demonstrate that Loki is a central figure in this conceptual system of Norse religion from the Viking Age. I will discuss how Loki affects society in the Norse world, focusing on the gender and sexuality of the god. Traditionally in scholarship, Loki has been identified as both bisexual and transformative in appearance—a hlúðr, or "shape-shifter". This analysis does not tend to consider conceptions of queerness as we understand them today, and uses a more conservative lens to comprehend the identity of Loki. I will argue, however, that this betrays a heteronormative bias and a reluctance to recognise queerness in ancient texts. My thesis attempts to shed light on the possibilities of queerness in early Norse societies. This topic is important, because while we acknowledge that gender and sexuality in ancient myth will have been understood differently, we can still consider it through a contemporary queer lens in order to reach new understandings of this topic.

For the purposes of this research, I am defining "mythology" as a reflection of the culture in which it was created, whose sets of beliefs, stories, and figures are passed down between the generations through oral and later written transmission. These traditions may have been modified as they travelled through time, in order to fit the thinking of the contemporary age. Mythology is part of, but does not exclusively represent, particular religious systems, and, by extension, a shared cultural heritage. While later Western concepts of mythology have tended to equate "myth" with falsity (as compared with Christian "truth"), we must remember its religious significance in the pre-Christian era and beyond.

In this broad definition of Norse myth, we find that the Norse conceptual model for both gender identities and gender roles is more complicated in its narrative. Other ancient cultures shared similar ideas to the Norse in how gender and sexuality are understood, although each culture has their unique way of accessing and understanding this knowledge. Using a comparative lens, we can develop an understanding of how religion and myth play a role in shaping societal beliefs about gender identity and sexuality.

## The world(s) of Norse Pagan mythology of the Viking Age

To understand the Norse Pagan religion, we must first understand the world it inhabits. The gods, elves, giants, dwarves, trolls, and humans live within a nine world or heim system. Humans live in the middle home named Miðgarð, or anglicised "Midgard," Middle Earth.

Surrounding this is a giant sea populated by one of the children of Loki, the Miðgarðsormr or Jormungandr, known as the Midgard Serpent. Fenrir, the wolf-child of Loki is chained on the boulder Gjöll, pushed into the centre of earth[73]. Giants live in Jotunheim, separated from the Frost giants who burst forth from Gunningagap, living at the edges of Midgard. The elves live in Alfheim, having separate areas for different types of elves; black elves, for instance, live underground. Trolls and goblins are similar

---

73. Young, Jean I, translator. *The Prose Edda of Snorri Sturluson: Tales from Norse Mythology.* Bowes and Bowes, 1954. p. 58.

to dwarves who can live in the ground as well, trapping weary humans in their holes or halls under the mountains.

The world of the deceased is made of innumerable halls, each one operated by a deity with the main halls being the hall of Freyja who takes women specifically slain from the battlefield, and, of course, Valhalla where warrior men go under the protection of Óðinn as the Einharjar.[74] These worlds or homes surround the life-tree, or world-tree, Yggdrásil. As in many cultures, this tree is made either of ash or yew and is immense. It is uncertain whether the tree represents a sort-of "highway" between the homes, or if its roots move into each home.

Movement exists horizontally and vertically between the nine homes. Hel, the daughter of Loki, lives in Niflheim[75]. Thor, Óðinn, and Frigg, alongside the other Æsir and Vanir, live in Ásgarð. In this place, Óðinn is king of the gods, or more rightly highest chief with many of the main gods exercising special gifts and having distinct personalities. Some gods live in other places, such as Skaði, a giantess who lives up in the mountains, and Njorðr, her sometime husband, who lives by the seas. We see these images on various archaeological stones or crosses, such as the Tjängvide picturestone depicting the eight-legged horse Sleipnir[76]:

## A note on the myths

All of these myths stem originally from oral histories. This means that by the time they were written down, largely collated by Snorri Sturluson in the 13th century from previous sources, they have been modified verbally. The extent to which the myths have been modified comes from one piece of surviving source material, the prose *Edda*, written by Snorri.

Here Snorri collated myths from earlier writings of the 10th to the 12th century. Being a Christian, some argument could be made for their Christianisation, especially in the myth *Gylfaginning*, which enshrines earlier stanzas of poetry (the transmission of the original myths) around a

---

74. Editor's note: Freyja's specific claim on women warriors and Odin's on men is the author's personal belief, rather than a concept based solely in lore.

75. Young, Jean I, translator. *The Prose Edda of Snorri Sturluson: Tales from Norse Mythology.* Bowes and Bowes, 1954. p. 56.

76. Image credit: Picture stone from Tjängvide, Alskog Parish, Gotland, Sweden. Wikimedia User Berig, Wikimedia Commons, CC BY-SA 4.0 rights, 1 March 2008. https://commons.wikimedia.org/wiki/File:Tjängvide.jpg

post-Christian narrative of King Gylfi. It is important to note that while the stanzas of surviving poetry from other sources may or may not be Christianised, they largely outline a Pagan premise. Our most complete understanding of Norse religion and its mythology stems from these surviving copies, particularly our fullest picture in the form of *Gylfaginning*.

The poem *Gylfaginning* was written in Iceland in the 13th century by Snorri Sturluson, using portions of oral history (as are most of the sagas). In this poem, we are given a description of Loki and their familial relationships:

> Also reckoned amongst the gods is one that some call the mischiefmonger of the Æsir and the father-of-lies and the disgrace-of-gods-and-men. He is the son of the giant Fárbauti and his name is Loki or Lopt. His mother's name is Laufey or Nál, and Byleist and Helbindi are his brothers. Loki is handsome and fair of face, but has an evil disposition and is very changeable of mood. He excelled all men in the art of cunning, and he always cheats. He was continually involving the Æsir in great difficulties and he often helped them out again by guile. His wife's name is Sigyn; their son Nari or Narvi.[77]

This poem offers us the most complete description of Loki in written form, and was written during the Medieval period. Its negative depiction of the god may therefore reflect the demonisation[78] of Loki that took place in the Christian era. We learn of these myths through the written transmission of oral mythology. There are also various pieces of archaeology, such as the Gotland picturestones and the Gosforth Cross, which also shed light on the myths of Loki.

To begin my interpretation of the role of Loki in the Norse religious system, and to answer my first thesis question, I will outline the systems of mythology suggested by Dumézil and the later argument put forward by Frakes on tripartism. Dumézil has written highly influential work on the Germanic mythology world, while Frakes is a prominent scholar of Norse literature. Both of these writers contribute significantly to under-

---

77. Young, Jean I., translator. *The Prose Edda of Snorri Sturluson: Tales from Norse Mythology.* Bowes and Bowes, 1954. p. 55.

78. Lindow, John. *Norse Mythology: A Guide to the Gods, Heroes, Rituals, and Beliefs.* Oxford University Press, 2002. p. 303.

standings of how the Norse religious system is constructed and understood as a whole.

## The role of Loki in Norse mythology: Dumézil

The work of scholar Georges Dumézil broke away from Max Müller's established theory of "solar theology,"[79] which asserted that the sun, amongst other agricultural phenomena, was the main deity in any given system. Dumézil created a new way to perceive the interconnections of Indo-European origins for Germanic mythology.

Drawing from the French Sociological School of 1938, Dumézil focused on comparative mythology under the direction of Durkheimian anthropology. Yet unlike Durkheim, the structural process (i.e. the categorising of gods and their functions) of his model is not linked to a collective underlying psycho-social understanding across all human beings, but rather is linked geographically as a familial collective to Indo-European boundaries.[80]

Dumezil argues that Germanic mythology has its origins in Indo-European mythology, and that mythology has specific familial or geographical roots. Dumézil also contends that various gods are counterparts to an earlier Indic tradition, confirming the influential migration of Scythians into Scandinavia during the Migration Period 300-700 CE. In this school of thought (French comparative mythology) of the forties and fifties, the way of thinking "asserts through the school that important social and cultural realities are '*collectively represented*' by supernatural beings and concepts, and that there is an intimate and functional connection between social facts and religious facts."[81]

With this methodological backdrop, Dumézil postulated in 1938 that the tripartite class system resembling the Aryan "twice born" caste system of Medieval and modern-day India[82] could be applied to various Indo-European mythological systems, including that of the Norse system more widely, and specifically to Germanic mythological systems.

---

79. Littleton, C. Scott. Introduction in Dumézil's *Gods of the Ancient Northmen*. University of California Press, 1973. p. x.

80. Dumézil, Georges. *Mitra-Varuna*. Presses Universitaires de France, 1940. p.16.

81. Littleton, C. Scott. Introduction in Dumézil's *Gods of the Ancient Northmen*. University of California Press, 1973. p. xi.

82. Ibid. p. x.

Dumézil published his newly revised system in two works, *Mitra-Varuna* (1940)[83] and *Jupiter, Mars & Quirinus* (1941)[84]. In these works, he postulated three points, or functions of the gods:

1) Maintenance of cosmic power by the gods
2) Exercise of physical prowess of the gods
3) Promotion of physical wellbeing by the gods

Georges Dumézil pioneered a new way of thinking about the Norse religious system, originally insisting that his tripartite system of gods was reflected in the social classes of Norse society. Twenty years later, however, he rescinded this claim. His basic premise was to group various deities in trios, to complement his tripartite function-related system. This meant the application of tripartism across the two groups of the Æsir and the Vanir, assimilated early on in the mythological timeframe. These two groups used to be at war with one another, until they exchanged hostages and assimilated into one group of gods.

Dumézil offers a unique way to understand Norse religion, positioning several key figures as a triad in his tripartite model.[85] For example, Óðinn, the chief of the gods, fulfils the role of maintaining cosmic power as a skilled magician. Þórr is positioned in the warrior class through the exercise of physical prowess. Njorð, with his son Frey, serve as the linkage to the third function, which is the promotion of physical well-being among the lowest classes. Within this tripartite construction, gods of the Æsir are held to be more significant than the Vanir.

The three gods most often utilised by Dumézil in this model are Óðinn, Þórr, and Frey, although occasionally Njorð is swapped out for Freyr, or his sister Freyja is placed in this position.[86] Dumézil was inspired by the three figurines reported by Medieval chronicler Adam of Bremen in his description of the temple at Uppsala, Sweden. Trios are often found in various Norse myths; however, as I will demonstrate, duos also make an appearance, such as Þórr and Loki who travel together on adventures. In

---

83. Dumézil, Georges. *Mitra-Varuna*. Presses Universitaires de France, 1940.
84. Dumézil, Georges. *Jupiter, Mars & Quirinus*. Gallimard, 1941.
85. Dumézil, Georges. *Gods of the Ancient Northmen*. Ed. Einar Haugen. University of California Press, 1973. p. 4.
86. Ibid. p. 4.

*Þórsdrápa*,[87] for example, Loki clings to Þórr's belt as they cross a river together, demonstrating Thor's strength and showcasing that the gods often rely on one another to carry out their adventures. My aim in this thesis is therefore to understand if and how Loki fits within the Dumézilian model. I also draw on the work of Frakes, who attempts to reconcile the position of Loki in the Dumézil system.

Dumèzil argues that triads are central to understanding Norse mythology because they link the myths to an Indo-European origin.[88] He also states that this system is recreated across society within three stages, or castes, likening these to the three-level caste system of Medieval India:

1) The varna, brahmana (priests)
2) The ksatriya (warriors)
3) The vaisya (breeder-farmers)

In this sense, Dumezil attempts to show that Germanic myth and religion has a tripartite system that can be traced back to Indo-European myth and religion. He bases his argument on the etymological links between languages and the comparative nature of the myths themselves despite their diversity.

For instance, Dumèzil creates a further schematic, drawing comparisons between Norse and Indic gods:[89]

1) Mitra and Varuna, the two sovereign gods
2) Ind(a)ra, who represents war and strength
3) The Nasatya, or Ásvin, twin gods representing youth, fertility, happiness, and health

This three-tiered pantheon aligns the Indo-European origins with Norse theology. In this argument, Dumézil organises deities into three groups, usually Óðinn, Þórr, and Freyr. Óðinn is linked to Mitra, Þórr to Ind(a)ra, and Freyr to Nasatya, or Ásvin. Dumézil assigns the second twin position to the father of Freyr, Njorð. This father-son combination changes the way this schematic plays out in the importance of the Vanir gods amongst the

---

87. Davidson, Hilda E. *The Lost Beliefs of Northern Europe.* Routledge, 2001. p. 80.
88. Ibid. p. 15.
89. Ibid. p. 16.

Æsir, utilising an older idea from Max Müller's "solar theology"[90] whereby these gods are demarcated as fertility agriculture deities. Dumezil argues that Norse myth is connected to Indic myth, so we can see connections between the gods and how they are organized in the pantheon (the functions they serve, etc). More rarely, the second twin or Mitra is likened by Dumézil to Freyr's sister Freyja. Dumézil argues that the identities of these Norse deities have been influenced by Zoroastrian Indo-Iranian, Indo-European traditions[91], then becoming through time the caste class system of Indic Medieval period. Dumézil uses this structuralist system to understand how the Germanic and Norse religious systems operated in form and function.

Dumézil postulates that the three-tiered system of gods reflects that of the society, calling upon Vedic examples to demonstrate this comparatively; he notes the differences in status between castes, and how this caste system is reflected in the Indic deity pantheon. Dumézil applies this notion of a caste system to the Norse gods, whom he splits into different social classes. Here, then, if we can match Loki into this system, we will see how they were understood to inform the social fabric of Norse society. I will argue that Loki's major role was to embody social queerness in the Viking Age.

However, in Dumézil's system, Loki is not considered a major god and is relegated under minor divinities in the pantheon, alongside Baldur and Heimdall. Loki and Heimdall fight to the death at the onset of Ragnarok, and according to Snorri, they take the form of seals.[92] The prime example for the nature of Loki also rests in the myth of the death of Baldur. These instances illuminate some important themes and will be discussed later. Loki sits within Dumézil's third-level structure alongside Freyja, whose role is similarly downplayed, despite the fact that her actions in various myths serve as a springboard for many of Loki's actions, which drive towards their fulfilling the destiny of Ragnarok.

These ideas about Loki from Dumézil's texts may have had their origin in the Migration Period (350-700 CE). In the Migration Period, we possibly see a merger of ideas and concepts in the form of oral history, whereby

---

90. Müller, Max. "Solar Theology". *Gifford Lectures of 1888-1892* (Collected Works, vols. 1-4), 1929.
91. Dumézil, Georges. *Gods of the Ancient Northmen*. Ed. Einar Haugen. University of California Press, 1973. p. 16-17.
92. Martin, John S. *Ragnarok: An Investigation into Old Norse concepts of the fate of the gods*. Royal VanGorcum Ltd., 1972. p. 81.

some ideas about the gods and their stories arose from the assimilation of the indigenous population and the incoming Indo-Europeans. This may be why in the Baldur death saga, *Baldurs draumar*, we see parallels with the myths of the *Mahabharata*. The demon Duryodhana bears some similarities to Loki in this myth, and there are also comparisons to be drawn between Hœdor and Dhrtarasta, both of whom are blind, and who defeat the seemingly invincible figures of Baldur and Yudhisthira respectively.

Dumézil's comparative readings of Indic and Norse mythology help us to understand the nature of Loki and how Loki fits within the pantheon of Norse gods. Loki is, in essence, an agent of chaos. This force of chaos can be found within other mythologies, which will be explored later. Nevertheless, Dumézil has not reconciled what I consider to be the most important part that Loki plays in Norse mythology: that is, his duality with Óðinn. Following Dumézil, I will use a comparative approach to explore the function of Norse gods, particularly Loki, in Norse society. However, I will propose a model of duality for the Norse pantheon. While I agree with Dumézil that Norse mythology reflects cultural and religious life in ancient Norse society,[93] I will attempt to modify his tripartite model to reflect the innate duality of the god Loki.

Dumézil explains that an independent Germanic system of mythology originated out of an Indo-European structure. The separation of deities into classes puts forth an independent class, the "Konr ungr" which takes on the aspects of magic and war. Dumézil posits that under the Indo-European system, magic and war were understood to be utilised differently across social classes of the gods.[94] This is also seen in the mythological system of the Egyptian gods Seth and Horus. Seth is not considered eligible for office of kingship as Horus is, but is still needed alongside the king in order to control the personified forces of chaos.[95] The king takes on the office of kingship, under the wings of Horus, to preserve the unity of the state and rein in the forces of chaos. Seth fulfils this second obligation for the king.

---

93. Ibid. p. 125.
94. Ibid. p. 125.
95. Te Vilde, H. *Seth, God of confusion: a study of his role in Egyptian mythology and religion.* Brill Publishing, 1967.

Dumézil, as noted by Littleton, tries to reconstruct past Indo-Europe-an society based on the three functions[96] operating towards a comparative mythological model. Yet this model leads to a lot of the gods in the pantheon of Germanic and Norse religion being relegated to minor or insignificant positions. To summarize then, Dumézil's model of Norse mythology assigns a social class to each god—priests, warriors and the masses (farmers, mostly). I agree with this typology, although it does not always attribute major roles to other deities who may have had a cult following.

Dumézil does identify Loki as a primary god but offers little detail about the substance which makes Loki "counted amongst the Æsir". This is the pitfall of the Dumézil model with regard to his understanding of major Norse deities. I therefore turn to the work of Frakes, who offers a more detailed exploration of Loki.

**Frakes**

First, I will explain how Frakes develops the Dumézil model to under-stand Norse religion. Frakes presents Loki as being ambiguous in nature[97]. He sets out to place Loki inside Dumézil's three-tiered model[98], but argues that in order to include Loki in the system, Dumézil's model has to be radically modified. Frakes suggests that Dumézil has utilised a Frazerian model of analysis, which means the traditional concept of comparing mythology across different cultures, but this model is now considered outdated[99].

Frakes argues that Loki plays a marginal role in the mythology[100], and therefore exists marginally in the mythological system. Loki plays an adjunct role amongst the main gods: "he is external to the system but is essential to its function, and thus it is as mediator between the outside and inside."[101] Frakes suggests that Loki takes on the negative aspects of Óðinn's functional tasks; Loki thus resembles the opposite of Óðinn in this system.

---

96. Littleton, C. Scott. *The New Comparative Mythology: An Anthropological Assessment of the Theories of Georges Dumézil.* 3rd Ed. University of California Press, 1982. p. 89.
97. Frakes, Jerald C. "Loki's Mythological Function in the Tripartite System" (*Lokasenna*). *The Poetic Edda: Essays on Old Norse Mythology.* Ed. Paul Acker & Carolyne Larrington. Routledge Publishing, 2002. p. 162.
98. Ibid. p. 163.
99. Ibid, p. 163.
100. Ibid. p. 165.
101. Ibid. p. 165.

Frakes furthermore states that Loki subverts the three functions represented by the Dumézil model (priestly countenance, justice, and fertility) by attacking the character of other gods in the myth of the *Lokasenna*.[102] In this myth, Loki stands in the hall of one of the other deities, and points out all the flaws of the gods as caricature. In doing so, Loki fulfils their role as opposition to the functions of the gods in the Dumézil model.

Also, according to Frakes, Loki subverts through actions and words the divine function of fertility: for example when they transform into a mare to woo Svaðilfœri the stallion. This opposes the divine functionality of the fertility gods, and in doing so they take this function over in a queer, and oftentimes sexual way. Here, Loki embodies the queerness of their actions, which plays out in their numerous "trickster" actions, a quality noted for this god, to which I will return.

In the selections of myth in the *Skáldskarpamál*, there is one myth about the weapons of the gods. Loki is responsible for equipping the gods with instruments[103] such as Mjöllnir, the hammer of Þórr, and Freyja's necklace, the Brisingàmen. Loki is therefore responsible for equipping the other gods so that they can perform the functions ascribed to them in the mythic system. Yet this gives Loki opportunities to subvert the norms of the system. According to Frakes, Loki does not belong within the three categories outlined by Dumézil. Indeed, Frakes suggests that Loki is at their most subversive when Baldur dies, as Baldur embodies all three functions of the Dumézil model:

1) The wisest of the gods
2) The most courageous in martial skill
3) The fairest of the gods

By being complicit in Baldur's death, Loki ensures that each of the other main gods are challenged in their functional role by Baldur's death, as Baldur had embodied all their various functions, providing an image of a three-in-one role. In this way, Loki creates a compelling marginality of the centre, whereby, as Frakes suggests, they represent the anti-functionary, who "mediates between them [the worlds] in both a positive and negative

---

102. Ibid. p. 168.
103. Ibid. p. 171.

sense, but he belongs to neither."[104]

In agreement with Frakes, I would argue that Loki is indeed essential to the mythological system, because they are counted amongst all the gods, and are the blood brother to Óðinn. Loki therefore, to quote Frakes, "represents the classic bind characteristic of sociological tension between the center and margin."[105] At this point, my interpretation must come to light.

## An alternative interpretation

In his discussion of Norse mythology, Frakes attempts to marry sociological conceptions of space and groupings, similar to anthropological "nodes and communities." In sociological terms, space is likened to a network of connections, forming groups of information or of people. I agree with his suggestion that Loki can inhabit both centre and margin. I further suggest that Loki does inhabit both spaces, as Frakes suggests, but *as part of their duality with* Óðinn.

I agree with Ström who puts forward the idea of Loki as a hypostasis of Óðinn[106], and also with Haugen,[107] who indicates that Loki represents a binary opposition against Óðinn. This is in part due to Loki being "blood brothers" with Óðinn. Loki, in my analysis, represents a key position in the Norse pantheon. In the Dumézil example of Vedic Mitra and Varuna, a contrast is created in the juxtaposition of dual sovereigns. This is the first tier accorded to the Tripartite system, where "the inner natures of the gods are clearly contrasted with one another."[108] Could this also be applied to the relationship, or duality, of Óðinn and Loki?

Both are diametrically opposed in natures. Both can indeed shape-shift, but differently from one another. Óðinn sends his consciousness out as other creatures, leaving his body lying somewhere as he "travels." Loki, on the other hand, physically changes gender and form. Both are deemed necessary by the other gods, the Æsir and Vanir, Óðinn being king or highest

---

104. Ibid. p. 171.
105. Ibid. p. 171.
106. Ström, Folke. "Loki: Ein mythologisches Problem," *Göteborg Universitets Årsskrift* 52.8. Elanders, 1956. p. 85.
107. Haugen, Einar. "The Mythical Structure of the Ancient Scandinavians: Some Thoughts of Reading Dumézil," *To Honor Roman Jakobson*. Jauna Linguarium, 32. Mouton, 1967. p. 863.
108. Ibid. p. 39.

chief, and Loki solving all of their problems—if these problems are not started by Loki in the first instance, of course—time and time again. They are "blood brothers," sealing the duality between the two. One is a god of poetry and war, the other skilled in oratory and craftiness. Both are cunning, in physicality and sexuality, both of them wittingly gaining what they need through trickery and enigmatic imagery. Surely, then, Loki deserves a greater role in the Norse pantheon than what they are granted by most scholars.

Loki becomes their own independent character in matters of preserving the gods when mischief is afoot. Specifically, Loki performs a dual function of both subverting *and* enabling the other gods' functions. Their enabling role is illustrated by their recollection of gifts they have given other gods: Iðunn's golden apples of youth, Óðinn's spear Grungnir, Mjöllnir given to Þórr in Þrymskviða, the forging of the gods' weapons in *Skáldskarpamál* such as Freyja's Brisingámen necklace, the Skiðblatnír ship for Frey which can be folded up and stowed in your pocket. Each of these gifts allows the gods to function in their given roles and empowers their identity. Therefore, their identities are created by Loki, owing to the specialised function of their equipment—especially Óðinn's spear Grungnir—each becoming integral to the nature of the god in recognising who they are. Loki proves again that they are central to the mythology and Norse religious system, by being a trickster who subverts the functions of the gods, but also enables the gods to perform their roles, as Frakes[109] insists.

Some sagas and poems also capture the essence of the trickster god, such as the *Saga of the Volsungs*.[110] In this saga, Loki kills Ottr with a rock, as Ottr takes on the form of an otter during the day. Unknown to Óðinn, Hœnir, and Loki, Ottr was the son of Hreidmar, and brother of Andvari and Fafnir (a dragon).[111] Hreidmar, on the death of Ottr, issues a challenge to fill the skin up with gold.[112] Ottr is then skinned, to be filled with the gold required as ransom for his death. Loki, who had killed Ottr, manages to collect all the gold by catching Andvari, who transforms into a pike, and

109. Frakes, Jerald C. "Loki's Mythological Function in the Tripartite System" (*Lokasenna*). *The Poetic Edda: Essays on Old Norse Mythology*. Ed. Paul Acker & Carolyne Larrington. Routeledge Publishing, 2002. p. 192.

110. Byock, Jesse, translator. *The Saga of the Volsungs: The Norse Epic of Sigurd the Dragon-Slayer*. University of California Press, 2012. p. 57-59.

111. Ibid. p. 57.

112. Ibid. p. 59.

dispenses gold via riddles. Loki then manages to repay Hreidmar for the death of his son, and because the gold was collected in the skin, it is named Ottr's Ransom.

This simple story demonstrates how Loki can create problems, but then is often the one charged with solving them—in their trickster capacity, they service the gods' desires, even when Loki receives no direct benefit from doing so. At other times, these challenges benefit both the other gods and Loki,[113] such as when Loki gets back the golden apples of Iðunn, giving the gods immortality again, after Loki bargained the apples away to a giant who had captured them. It is this bargaining and slyness which Loki is often known for, but we can also see how Loki's nature is different from that of the other gods.

Other scholars have attempted to position Loki as a lesser character, such as De Vries who states that Loki is a "ganz eine Satanische Gestalt" (a wholly Satanic character).[114] Likewise, Anne Holtsmark[115] diminishes Loki by suggesting they are a simple court jester character. I contend that Loki is in fact a pivotal character in the pantheon, who sets up the destiny which follows the gods in their exploits. These scholars limit the extent to which Loki inhabits the worlds of the gods, and their central role in claiming destiny in the events leading up to, and during, Ragnarok.

Loki, for all intents and purposes, can and does fulfil the requirements of being a major god. For instance, Loki always accompanies the main gods, particularly Þórr, engineers the decisive weaponry and accoutrements of the gods, and, as Frakes states, inverts the collective system. I would also add that Loki in their duality achieves the destined end of their role and function—that of Ragnarok. This is an impressive god who stands out above several figures in the mythology, and it is to this end that we must contemplate the most sacred of roles they perform in this fulfilment.

We come to the most important *þáttr* (episode) regarding the god Loki: that is, the death of Baldur. Baldur is the son of Óðinn, and is the handsomest of the gods, with blond, flowing hair. He is also very fair and just, often portrayed as being the most righteous of the gods. Baldur is also

113. Dronke, Ursula. *Myth and Fiction in Early Norse Lands.* Variorum, 1996. p. 13.
114. De Vries, Jan. *Altgermanische Religionsgeschichte, II.* Walter de Gruyter & Co., 1957. p. 262.
115. Holstmark, Anne. *Norrøn mytologi: Tro og myter i Vikingtiden.* Det Norske Samlaget, 1976. p. 155.

impervious to weapons of any kind, including rocks and stones. This is because the goddess Frigg got every inanimate object to swear that they would not hurt Baldur. This was done to all objects except one small plant, the mistletoe. Loki uses this to their advantage in order to bring about Baldur's death, but I argue that they recognise their role in this event is for a greater purpose, rather than one performed out of malice. They therefore conspire to set in motion the Twilight of the Gods, Ragnarok.

Ragnarok is a necessary destiny for the gods, which Loki enables. To do this, Loki needs to learn the weakness of Baldur, and so, disguises themselves as a woman to ask Frigg about Baldur's invulnerability. Frigg lets slip that she did not ask the mistletoe because it was only a very young plant at the time. Thus, Loki gains knowledge of what will kill Baldur. The gods would usually play a game when gathered for the Thing (meeting), whereby they would throw various weapons and items at Baldur and watch them bounce off his body, not harming him. As this game is played, Loki approaches the blind god Höðr, who normally would not play as he cannot see. Loki whispers to him that he should throw something at Baldur (unknown to Höðr, this is mistletoe), and points the god in the right direction, so he can participate in the game. Hœdor then unwittingly throws the mistletoe at Baldur, and it pierces his body, killing him.[116]

Baldur is given a proper funeral, atop a pyre, where Óðinn whispers a secret into the ear of his dead son. Baldur is now in Niflheim, the realm of the goddess Hel, a daughter of Loki. To try and revive his son, Óðinn[117] visits Hel, who rules over the dead who die outside of battle. Hel will only relinquish Baldur if everything of the world weeps for him: all the stones, trees, and creatures. All do so except one, an old giantess—who, according to Snorri, is none other than Loki transformed—and in doing so, denies the return of Baldur to the living (until Ragnarok passes).

The gods soon learn of the trick that Loki has played. Eventually, Óðinn and the other gods bind Loki up in chains or snakes in a cave,[118] (see image from the Gosforth Cross on p. XXXX) leaving them to be dripped upon

---

116. Terry, Patricia. *Poems of the Elder Edda.* University of Pennsylvania Press, 1990. p. 241-244.

117. Editor's note: Or, in some versions of this tale, Hermod, Baldr's brother.

118. Young, Jean I. *The Prose Edda of Snorri Sturluson: Tales From Norse Mythology.* Bowes and Bowes, 1954. p. 85.

by poison oozing from the rock above their head.[119] This is reminiscent of Loki visiting the giant Utgardr-Loki, who is also bound underground in chains.[120] Perhaps this is Loki visiting their mythic-future self. As this myth unfolds, Loki has already committed the acts of the *Lokasenna* where he jokes at the other gods' expense. This myth then follows, in a chronology of myths, the beginning of Ragnarok. I argue that Loki realises their mythic destiny in ushering in Ragnarok, and thereby fulfils their sacred position as controller of chaos. An alternative consequence of the *Lokasenna* is that Loki is bound by the intestines of their son Narfi.[121]

Loki is bound as a consequence of the *Lokasenna*. The additional comments of Loki being bound in a cave is attested in *Völuspá*, amongst other poems, such as *Gylfaginning* and *Hauksbók*.[122] Olrik compares Loki to a chain-bound monster, blaming Loki for the beginnings of Ragnarok, and likens them to Prometheus of the Greek tradition.[123] This is potentially shown in mythic relief work on the Gosforth Cross monument. This occurs after the death of Baldur in the mythic chronology.

The events surrounding the death of Baldur are mentioned by Dumézil to reflect another Indo-European myth, the *Mahabharata*.[124] What makes the Baldur myth relevant to us is not only that it demonstrates the significance of Loki's trickery, but also shows how Loki again changes gender, on no less than two occasions. This is unlike the god Óðinn who changes form into various creatures whilst retaining his gender identity as male.

Loki has no qualms about changing gender and could be perceived as being gender fluid in nature. They change form into an old lady, and a giantess, freely abandoning a fixed gender role in these instances, which champions the idea of gender fluidity in form. This ties in with the

119. Faulkes, Anthony. *Gylfaginning (Edda & Prologue)*. Clarendon Press, 1982.
120. Lindow, John. *Norse Mythology: A Guide to the Gods, Heroes, Rituals, and Beliefs*. Oxford University Press, 2002. p. 302.
121. Terry, Patricia. *Lokasenna* in *Poems of the Elder Edda*. Philadelphia University Press, 1990. p. 83.
122. Lindow, John. "Myth and Mythography" in *Old Norse-Icelandic Literature: A Critical Guide*. Ed. Lindow, John and Clover, Carol J. University of Toronto Press, 2005. p. 31.
123. Olrik, A. *Der gefangene Riese im Kaukasus*. Germany, 1922. p. 133-276.
124. Dumézil, Georges. *Gods of the Ancient Northmen*. Ed. Einar Haugen. University of California Press, 1973. p. 64.

*Þrymskviða* or *Lay of Thrym.*

In this myth, the hammer of Þórr, Mjöllnir, has been taken by the giant Þrym. Loki is sent to gather it for Þórr, as is usually Loki's role to solve the problems of the gods. Loki reports after a brief visit to Þrym that to get the hammer back, the giant wishes to be married to the goddess Freyja. This of course will not do, as Freyja is the most beautiful of all the Æsir. A plan forms to dress Þórr up as Freyja in bridal costume, and Loki immediately suggests that they go along too as a bridesmaid. Loki and Þórr are so convincing that as they attend the ceremony, the hammer is brought out and Þórr once again claims it, at which point he kills Þrym and his followers.[125] Here, Loki assumes a female identity immediately, whereas Þórr had to be convinced. This willing gender fluidity of Loki stands in stark contrast to the hyper-masculinity of Þórr.

At times, Loki seems to be confirming gender and sexual binaries by having (female) wives and creating three monster offspring by the ogress Angrboda: the Midgard Serpent (Jormungandr), Fenris the giant wolf, and Hel, ruler of the underworld at Niflheim. Loki also has two sons by their wife Sigyn named Nari and Narfi,[126] neither of whom seem to be mentioned during Ragnarok, curiously. The sons of Þórr, however, are mentioned and reclaim their father's mighty hammer after the end of days, in a renewal event. At this event we are reminded that Loki has already killed Baldur as mentioned in *Baldrs draumar*,[127] and now must lead into the *Lokasenna* for their final act before the destiny in Ragnarok—Loki as an instigator of chaos rebalances the cosmos.

Dumézil mentions that because Loki does not have a cult, or various places named after them, such as Þórr might have, they do not have a function[128] within the tripartite system. This is not so. Various other deities in the pantheon do not have places named after them, or visible signs of cultic activity. For instance, the goddess Jord has a sacred site mentioned in the poems, but is not a central actor in the death of Baldur, which is considered arguably to be one of the most important myths in the pantheon of Ger-

---

125. Terry, Patricia. *Poems of the Elder Edda*. Philadelphia University Press, 1990. p. 85-89.

126. Editor's note: Some myth versions also suggest Vali is a name for one of these two sons with Sigyn.

127. Terry, Patricia. *Baldrs draumar* (stanzas 8-10) in *Poems of the Elder Edda*. Philadelphia University Press, 1990. p. 242.

128. Dumézil, Georges. *Loki*. Les Dieux et les hommes, 1. G.P. Maissonnouve, 1948.

manic and Norse religion. Davidson attests that there are but three deities actively worshipped in a cult: Óðinn, Þórr, and Freyr. Others, including Loki, appear cult-less, going by the lack of reference to their worship in the body of literature that survives.

The idea of Loki and others without cult worship is only circumstantial due to our lack of available source evidence. Loki could indeed have had a cult just as Freyja almost certainly did,[129] yet the real importance of having a cult is not an important factor in whether a god was important or not. Loki has been shown as an important figure in the mythology, and yet no evidence appears of a cult. There perhaps is no real need for a physical cult if a god's status went beyond requiring a place of worship; this further attests to Loki's fluidity—they are not pinned down to one place or space in terms of worship. Even so, monuments attest to the myths of Loki. For instance, on the Gosforth Cross, Cumbria (note fig. above), Loki is shown in one scene bound and with the poison dripping upon them. As Davidson points out,[130] this myth is attested in the written literature of *Gylfaginning*, stanza 51.5-10—*ok urðu þau bond at járni*[131]—"and these bonds became iron."

In the myths associated with Loki, oftentimes geographic details are presented on the various trips that Loki makes with other gods. This is important as it consolidates the Norse worldview, showing how the gods interact with their societies, and in particular how Loki is viewed as being counted amongst the Æsir. Geographically, Loki is bound in chains nearby to the river Slíðr (Fearful),[132] which Saxo Grammaticus suggested contained weapons.[133]

In the myth of *Völuspá*,[134] we get a brief glimpse into the pain of Loki bound in the cave, during stanza 34: *Hapt sá hón liggia undir Hveralundi,*

---

129. McKinnell, John. "Some Basic Considerations" in *Both One and Many: Essays on Change and Variety in Late Norse Heathenism*. Philologia, 1994. p. 1.
130. Davidson, Hilda E. *Lost Beliefs of Northern Europe*. Routledge, 2001. p. 50.
131. Faulkes, Anthony. *Gylfaginning (Edda & Prologue)*. Clarendon Press, 1982. p. 49.
132. Ibid. p. 67.
133. Davidson, Hilda E. "Commentary on Saxo Grammaticus" in *History of the Danes I-IX* (Volume 2). Woolbridge, 1980.
134. Jónsson, Finnur. *Völuspá*, stanza 34. *Sæmundr Edda: Eddukvæði*. Prentsmiðja D. Östlunds, 1905. p. 11.

*lægiarn líki Loka áppekkian* or "A captive she saw lying under Cauldron's Grove, in the shape of malignant Loki, unmistakable."[135]

This is important because it demonstrates the pain Loki is willing to endure as a consequence of meeting their destiny. What came as a footnote to the poem *Lokasenna*[136] attests that Loki is bound under a poisonous snake from which their wife Sigyn captures the poison in a bowl. When Sigyn goes to empty the bowl, Loki writhes in the form of earthquakes. This scene is related to ideas of Utgard-Loki being a Prometheus character in Greek mythology: Prometheus gave fire to humanity, Loki instead gives a renewal of the world.

The geographic details provided in these myths help consolidate the Norse worldview. The people could visualise where these places were, and attest to their place name or function when they saw fit to "find" these sacred places. For example, the idea of a bound god is attested across other cultural identities such as the Greek myth of Prometheus, and the writhing of a bounded Loki creating earthquakes may have originated from south-eastern Europe[137] in the Caucasus mountains, where Prometheus was held. Loki in this guise as Utgard-Loki may have then been transmitted through oral histories by the Greeks or perhaps even from merchants. Therefore, areas of myth locations would hold a special meaning to the society, and so the location of Loki being bound would be an important aspect of the myth. Geography, then, consolidates the Norse worldview.

It is in this consolidation of the Norse worldview that we can begin to fully understand the nature of Loki. In relation to Frakes, we need to understand the binary conception of a duality. Here, two opposing representatives make up the balancing of chaos and good, although being chaotic is not necessarily considered to be evil as such, but a challenge to the system. According to De Vries, Loki does not willingly engage in actions that will benefit the gods, but is instead forced to do so.[138] I would argue that Loki is the only one who can solve the problems of the gods and therefore is again counted as one of the gods, whether Loki creates these problems or not. It

---

135. Dronke, Ursula. *The Poetic Edda: Volume II: Mythological Poems*. Clarendon Press, 1997. p. 16.

136. Lindow, John. *Norse Mythology: A Guide to the Gods, Heroes, Rituals, and Beliefs*. Oxford University Press, 2001. p. 213.

137. Davidson, Hilda E. *The Viking Road to Byzantium*. Routledge, 1976. p. 313.

138. De Vries, Jan. "Loki. . . Und kein Ende" in *Festschrift für Franz Rolf Schröder zu seinem 65*. Geburtstage, ed. Wolfdietrich Rasch, 1959. p. 9.

is nonetheless part of their role in the system of mythology. Loki does not conform to one form or function, but instead queers both of these aspects, while being fluid in that they create *and* solve problems.

Interestingly, Schjødt further likens Loki to a god "who either was inspired by Christianity or was a product of the conceptions and fantasy of late pagan poets".[139] Owing to the lack of sources we have and the difficulty in relying on them, it is impossible to determine which of these options is correct. Schjødt[140] seeks to identify Loki as a degenerate quality of mythological life, moving from the helper of the gods to their chief antagonist. In doing so, Loki is showing the inevitable journey towards Ragnarok. I would agree that Loki is indeed the gods' helper, but serves as an antagonist in order to fulfil destiny, and thus serves in their role as a duality of the system.

Like Frakes, I would argue that Loki disrupts the mythological system and takes on the three functional qualities put forward by Georges Dumézil, all the while subverting them. By doing so, Loki is enacting the path toward Ragnarok in mythic future tense. It is by Loki's hand that the functions of the gods are attacked, and by killing Baldur, Loki has put in motion the sequence of Ragnarok as stated in the pre-Christian myth *Völuspá*. This myth depicts a seeress, the Volva, recounting her sacred knowledge after being called up by Óðinn to learn more wisdom. The wisdom she speaks of is in many of the myths already mentioned here, ending in an account of Ragnarok. It is a detailed account of all the events associated with Ragnarok, including Loki steering the ship laden with differing evils to fight the gods.[141] It is this precise action, an action Loki allows to happen and in fact takes control of, which highlights their ultimate destiny—to bring about the destruction of order, and to rebalance the cosmos.

Loki's attack in the pre-Christian myth *Lokasenna* therefore shows how the gods have become lazy, incompetent, and shirking of their responsibilities as functionaries to the system. It is through this timeline that Loki is bound and left to have poison drip onto their body, showing the suffering they need to endure in order to meet their destiny. The final section of Ragnarok is the rebirth of the world, with humans Lif and Lifthrasir emerging from the Yggdrásil tree to repopulate the earth. Baldur also re-

---

139. Schødt, Jens P. "Om Loke endnu engang" in *ANF* 96:49-86:49, 1981.
140. Ibid. p. 80-84.
141. Ibid. p. 6.

turns from Hel, resurrected in an almost Christ-like fashion. This is the destiny that Loki instigates—a re-emergence of order from the bounds of chaos—and it is only Loki who could produce this; no other god, save for Heimdall, could do so.

Heimdall is mentioned only because he embodies all three functions as Baldur does, and fittingly, he comes to his death by combatting Loki, who also dies in this fight during Ragnarok. The duality with Óðinn, and now Heimdall here, is astounding. Heimdall and Loki are both opposites to each other in function and form, ending their respective lives going up against one another. Interestingly, in the *Hauksbók* version of the poem, the emphasis is placed on warfare as the cause of Ragnarok, rather than through the death of Baldur.[142]

The pre-Christian myth of Loki and Iðunn with her golden apples also clearly demonstrates the nature of the god as a charming and intelligent trickster. There are two accounts of this myth: an incomplete version in *Haustlong*, and the more in-depth treatment of *Skáldskarpamál* by Snorri Sturluson, writing in the 13th century CE. The story goes that Óðinn, Loki, and Hœnir grow hungry on a trip, and so take a cow from a nearby farm. It does not cook on the fire as they expect it to, and so an eagle sitting atop a tree offers to cook the meat in exchange for a share in the portions left. The meat is cooking when the eagle takes off with most of the meat! Loki, seeing this, grabs a stick to try and retake the carcass, and instead finds themselves stuck onto the stick they whacked the meat with, dragged under the eagle, high above the clouds. The eagle reveals his identity as Thjazi, a giant king, who is not going to let Loki go unless they bargain for something. Loki grows wise to this and agrees to deliver Iðunn to his home, with the golden apples of immortality.

Returned to Ásgarð, Loki lures the innocent Iðunn out of the hall, at which point Thjazi, waiting as an eagle, scoops her up in his claws and carries her off. Soon after this, the gods notice something is wrong. They each begin ageing, covered with wrinkles, and immediately see the guilt Loki carries. A heated debate occurs and Loki is threatened with death unless they manage to return Iðunn and her apples. Loki borrows Freyja's feather cloak, transforming themselves into a falcon, and then flies to Jotunheim,

---

142. Lindow, John. "Mythology and Mythography" in Clover, Carol J. Clover and Lindow, John, editors, *Old Norse-Icelandic Literature: A Critical Guide*. University of Toronto Press, 2005. p. 31.

the home of the Jotnar, or giants. Loki then transforms Iðunn into a nut (maybe an acorn), and carries her under their wings back to Ásgarð.

The gods back at Ásgarð create a bonfire in which Thjazi, when chasing Loki back home, singes his wings as Loki sweeps and flips in and out of danger. The singeing of Thjazi's wings means he falls into Asgard, flightless. The gods take this opportunity to kill the giant, now that Iðunn is safely back.

This myth shows the nature of Loki as not just a trickster, but a trickster who is intelligent, charming, and intuitive. It also showcases Loki's heroism. This can be seen in the rescuing of Iðunn, something that Loki was adamant to do after experiencing guilt upon sending her away—otherwise, they too would have perished due to the loss of Iðunn's apples of immortality.

This myth also shows Loki and Óðinn moving around worlds accompanied by a third figure (in this case, Hœnir). This trio pattern is repeated in many of the myths of Loki and Þórr, pushing against the argument that presupposed Óðinn, Þórr, and Freyr as the three tripartite gods of the system. Here, we see Loki being included in this system of trios in ways that at times benefit the gods—such as giving them their equipment and weaponry which hone their identities—or potentially harm the gods, such as when Loki lets Thjazi take Iðunn and her golden apples. This shows us the full complexity of the character of Loki, and in doing so paints a picture that is far more complex than the title "trickster god." Instead, Loki is shown to express different behaviours and emotions, such as fear, guilt, and bravery, and to behave with both honour and dishonour in relation to the other gods, who at times threaten Loki with death.

Another feature of the adventures Loki performs is highlighted by Jacob Grimm, who likens Loki to the elemental position of fire[143] and compares them to the god Hephæstus of Greek mythology. Both are extricated from the group of gods, and both are chained up, as is Loki's son Fenrir.[144] This is also linked to the myth of Utgardr-Loki, which features an eating contest in which the god Loki is pitted against the elemental fire of Logi, who of course beats Loki in the actual competition. Grimm conflates Logi and Loki and suggests Loki is related to the element of fire due to them being

143. Grimm, Jakob. *Teutonic Mythology.* Translator Stallybrass, J.S. 4th edition. Dover Publications Ltd., 1989. p. 241.
144. Ibid. p. 241.

a brother of Hlér (water) and Kari (air), to which this Logi (fire) is a third brother.[145] This trio allows us to understand Loki as potentially relating to the Æsir whilst existing as a separate entity. Grimm[146] also makes sense of the blood brothership, locating the name of Óðinn as perhaps being related etymologically to the words óð (sense) and önd (breath and spirit).[147] This means that, as elements, Loki and Óðinn could be related, due to the elemental nature of the name Óðinn and the relation of Loki as the fire element. But what do other scholars say about the nature of Loki?

McKinnell's thesis appears to substantiate my own, utilising the Claude Lévi-Strauss theorem of mythology: "a strictly contemporary witness to social conditions at the time of preservation."[148] According to McKinnell, myths are created by binary oppositions to social settings—such as good versus evil, Æsir versus Jótunn. According to Lévi-Strauss, these mediators, or oppositions, can take on multiple oppositions that can lead to an even deeper understanding of a particular mediator.[149] Moreover, all the oppositions will ultimately reflect one central binary opposition. McKinnell contends that the basic binary opposition is between civilisation and chaos, embodied by the gods and the forces of Ragnarok. Loki is regarded in this system as being both a destabilising influence in the universe and a heroic saving character.[150] This suggests that Loki is a balancer of order and chaos, and McKinnell suggests that Loki balances these forces precariously.[151]

This is similar to my own view, except I propose that Loki is part of a duality system with Óðinn, given their blood brother relationship, and that Loki is counted amongst the Æsir. With this in mind, binary oppositions can play a role in any duality, but in this case, it is complicated by the nature of the god Loki and their role in perpetuating the destiny that is

---

145. Editor's note: While the direct Logi-Loki conflation is generally not upheld by current scholarship, the connections between the two nonetheless have significance, as they permeate folklore and modern practice.

146. Ibid. p. 242.

147. Ibid. p. 242.

148. Orton, Peter. "Pagan Myth and Religion" in *A Companion to Old Norse-Icelandic Literature and Culture.* McTurk, R., editor. Blackwell Publishing Ltd., 2005. p. 314.

149. Lévi-Strauss, Claude. "The Structural Study of Myth" in *Myth: A Symposium.* Sebeok, T. A., editor. Indiana University Press, 1958. p. 81-106.

150. McKinnell, John. *Both One and Many: Essays on Change and Variety in Late Norse Heathenism.* Philologia 1, 1994. p. 37.

151. Ibid. p. 37.

Ragnarok. Loki is not necessarily on the side of good or evil; they operate, as Frakes mentions, in a way that is both inside and outside the system. The position of Loki inside and outside the system is touched upon by Margaret Clunies-Ross. She uses the Lévi- Straussian model to explain early Scandinavian thought[152] to which "the mythic world encodes" social norms and behaviours.[153] Loki is demonised in later thought, and, through the preservation of these oral histories,[154] the Christian writers may have wanted to portray Loki as being evil by going against the social norm. In this sense, Loki impacts Norse society in a queer reading, which I discuss further in the next section.

**Loki and Norse society: How duality empowers Norse society and Loki's central position**

Hilda Ellis Davidson suggests that the Norse gods reflect approved human behaviours, stating that humans "valued traditional laws which were believed to have been established by the gods they worshipped."[155] Yet these types of portrayals tend to define the nature of Loki differently, offering no full explanation of the god, including their sexuality and gender identity, which are often repressed or avoided.

Traditional laws reflected social norms and could promote a sense of unity within a community. Perhaps these norms are built into the myths, and by extension, the standing stones which commemorate them. For example, upon the Alskog Tjängvide stone in Gotland, the horse Sleipnir is depicted with Óðinn atop (as shown earlier). This confirms the known myth of the building of the walls of Ásgarð, in which the union of Loki and Svaðilfœri the stallion produced Sleipnir. In the myth, Loki changes form and gender to a horse, a mare, and actually gives birth to Sleipnir. This is mentioned in the myth of *Gylfaginning,* and the horse Sleipnir is also found in a description of *Völuspá.* This is mythical confirmation in stone of Loki's changing gender as well as their pansexuality. This gender and sexual

152. Clunies-Ross, Margaret. *Prolonged Echoes: Old Norse Myths in Medieval Northern Society.* Odense Publishing, 1994.

153. Ibid. p. 34.

154. Orton, Peter. "Pagan Myth and Religion" in *A Companion to Old Norse-Icelandic Literature and Culture.* McTurk, R., editor. Blackwell Publishing Ltd., 2005. p. 316.

155. Davidson, Hilda E. *Scandinavian Mythology.* Hamlyn, 1982. p. 8.

fluidity does not create tension amongst the other gods, but rather appears to be simply accepted.

Queerness is mentioned directly in relation to Loki; for instance, Frigg recounts in her prophetic wisdom the travesties of Loki and Óðinn (*Lokasenna* 25). In this, we see the complexity of Loki in that they perform their trickster capacities similar to those of the Egyptian god Seth, and we can see that Loki is more than a mere trickster. They have an eschatological role in the formation of the mythic past, present and definitively its future (at Ragnarok).

In the myths of the ancient Egyptians, the god Seth is identified as a trickster deity and brother to the office of kingship god Horus.[156] Seth can be regarded as the charismatic and knowledgeable god of chaos. Yet, if we see images of the god in Egyptian contexts, we may struggle to identify what species Seth is. Seth can be identified with at least 20 different species, ranging from a pig to a fish. Within the writing system of ancient Egypt, Seth was used as a determiner alongside the Egyptian words for "storm," "tumult," and other aspects of cosmic social changes. As an agent of Egyptian duality, Seth transforms the conception of normality and makes real the ideas of mystery and change.

Régis Boyer notes that Loki is an anti-hero, a negative counterpart or parodic figure in mythology.[157] This role aligns closely to that of the god Seth in Egyptian mythology. Seth, like Loki, is always fraught with situations, or at least making sure things do not go as planned. Both are related to the opposition of kingship, and yet serve this kingship in balance—as both are necessary to equalise the world, in the duality of order (Horus, or Óðinn). In essence, both of these gods form a duality—which is very strongly evident in Egyptian culture.

**Findings**

Through these examples, Loki is conceptually similar in nature and function to Seth. With this in mind, we can make sense of the identities and ways-of-being in the Norse conceptions of gender. In the descriptions and lore surrounding the god Loki, we find a parallel definition of gender

---

156. Te Velde, Herman. "Seth" in *The Oxford Encyclopedia of Ancient Egypt*. Redford, D., editor. Oxford University Press, 2001.

157. Dumézil, Georges. *La religion des anciens Scandinaves*. Payot, 1981. p. 134.

fluidity and neutrality. Mirroring Seth, Loki is generally given male-identified pronouns, and similarly to the god Seth in ideas of form, we can see in Loki an appearance that is not always stable or immediately apparent to a known gender form.

What makes Loki exceptional in Norse religion is that their acceptance is deliberately categorised and identified by the Æsir and by the 13th century compiler of Norse mythology, Snorri Sturluson. In agreement with John Lindow,[158] I believe that one of the most significant lines characterizing Loki's personality is "Sá er enn talðr með Ásum" or "That one who is for ever counted amongst the gods."[159]

This line from *Gylfaginning,*[160] in Snorri Sturluson's *Edda*, is seen by Lindow as an inclusion of Loki into the fold of the gods, despite breaking patrilineal notions of belonging. In this sense Loki—whose father was a giant named Fárbauti, and mother Laufey or sometimes Nál—being one of the Æsir, should not count. Jakobsson[161] states that many of the familial relations to the Æsir are through a patrilineal connection. Loki's relation to the Æsir through their mother shows a change to the more traditional Viking belief that your status comes from the relation to your father. This means that Loki subverts the norm by having a potential Æsir as mother and a Jotun as father, thereby queering patrilineal traditions.

Furthermore, I would argue that Loki symbolises extended gender identity and sexuality concepts within Norse society. The context surrounding the shape-shifting forms of Loki derives primarily from the Norse conception of *hljuðð*, or "shape-shifting". For the Norse, this is connected deeply to an understanding of identity. Loki takes the forms of several animals and genders at will, often to further an objective in which Loki would benefit. For example, in the myth *Gylfaginning* is mentioned the story of the building of Ásgarð's walls. Loki woos Svarðilfari by taking the form of a mare—a female horse—in order to obstruct the builder's ability to complete his task. In this, Loki become impregnated and soon gives birth to the eight-legged horse Sleipnir. Loki turns into a mare, changing form and gender,

158. Lindow, John. *Norse Mythology: A Guide to the Gods, Heroes, Rituals, and Beliefs.* Oxford University Press, 2001. p. 216.
159. Author's own translation. Stanza from: Faulkes, Anthony. *Gylfaginning and Prologue.* Clarendon Press, 1982.
160. Ibid. p. 26.
161. Jakobsson, Ármann. "The Patriarch: Myth & Reality" in *Youth and Age in the Medieval North.* Lewis-Simpson, S., editor. Brill Publishing, 2008.

to woo the stallion—who is male—allowing a subversion of gender and therefore a queer reading in this myth. In social contexts, this shapeshifting phenomenon is thought to be present when you are a legendary Berserker upon the battlefield, who becomes as enraged as a bear, or when your spiritual guardian and avatar is shown as an animal to those who see you.

DuBois, however, comments that Loki is a trickster-demon of Christianised writing,[162] which various scholars also attest to in their writings. Lönnroth argues for a 13th century Icelander reception of the contemporary edition of *Völuspá*, and how this premise can be echoed in the Viking Age with regards to its Pagan core, rather than its Christian additions.[163] I would argue that in this Norse context, the attribution of male-identified pronouns for this god were an effect of Christianisation and that the original (fluid) gender norms are replaced during the Christian era. I also contend that what is present in the 13th century was ultimately cemented in place for and by post-Pagan writers as a product of their Romanized Christian faith. Christian influences across the Eddic poems must be recognised. Some scholars, such as Lönnroth, have pointed out we are possibly reading mythology in its Christianised and heavily redacted form.

The contemporary concerns and fully Christianised understanding of what it is to be a moral, and indeed good, Norse people during the northern Middle Ages has resulted in the written transmission of oral mythology. In the potentially pre-Christian myth of *Lokasenna*, recorded after Christianity, Loki mocks the gods, and in return, invites negative reactions, to the point where Loki is charged with counts of *ergi* (sexual perversion) and unmanliness alluded to in the stanzas: ". . . but you spent eight years beneath the earth, a woman, milking cows, and bearing babies! that I call craven"[164] and ". . . but I find it strange to see among us a god who gave birth to babies."[165]

This is a critical queer reading of how Loki engenders their sexuality, at times for the good of the gods, such as when turned into a mare to stop the master builder from winning a bet, or when accompanying Þórr to claim

162. DuBois, Thomas A. *Nordic Religions in the Viking Age.* University of Pennsylvania Press, 1999. p. 50.

163. Lönnroth, Lars. "Tesen om de två kulturerna: Kritiska studier i den isländska sagaskrivningens sociala förutsättningar" in *Scripta Islandica* 15. 1964. p. 1-97.

164. Terry, Patricia. "The Insolence of Loki: Locasenna," stanza 23 in *Poems of the Elder Edda.* University of Pennsylvania Press, 1990. p. 76.

165. Ibid. p. 78.

his hammer back. However, in this case, Loki is attributed to giving birth to their three monstrous children (Jormungandr, Hel, and Fenrir), who ultimately play out the destiny of Ragnarok. Loki's queerness, by giving birth, is both disruptive but plays a key role in the destiny of the gods. It is both necessary and functional.

*Lokasenna* is positioned by Sveinsson as being composed around 1000 CE,[166] and may be a late Pagan or post-Conversion myth, as the laws of *ergi* were codified after the introduction of the Christian church in Iceland (where Snorri writes) by the year 1000, in the lawbook *Grágas*. This still betrays an acknowledgement that Loki is key, and indeed necessary to, queerness in a post-Conversion worldview.

*Nið*, a term referring to a sexual perversion law in the 13th century, is also considered a charge of unmanliness, but oftentimes refers to a duel rather than an outright charge of sexual misconduct. It builds upon the hyper-masculinity of the 13th century Medieval Christian Icelandic world and as such this term as itself may not necessarily be attributed to the Viking period. This is pivotal in analysing Loki as a queer character and a queer role model in Norse society. The evidence against this being morally acceptable is developed by a Christian rather than Pagan audience, who would not have celebrated or encouraged such understandings of gender and sexuality within society. It clearly must have been acceptable, or at the very least tolerated amongst the Norse if it had to be banned by later Christian tradition.

Judy Quinn discusses the post-Christian myth *Hyndluljóð*, arguing that Loki's transformation into a female, who becomes pregnant after having sex with an evil woman and gives birth to all the witches and evils of the world, signifies what Quinn deems condemning "lesbianism". Loki's transformation into a birthing mother is therefore an act of subversion.[167] This means that by having two women making offspring and giving birth we arrive at a subversion of 13th century understandings of gender norms and practices, which may in the Viking period have been acceptable in this context. If we read this in a queer guise, this act of two women having sex may appear to be portrayed in a negative light (given the outcome).

166. Sveinsson, Einar. *Lokasenna*. Almenna Bókafelagið, 1962. p. 21.

167. Quinn, Judy. "Women in Old Norse Poetry and Sagas" in *A Companion to Old Norse-Icelandic Literature and Culture*. McTurk, R., editor. Wiley-Blackwell, 2005. p. 524.

However, the myth hints at rape when Loki shapeshifts into a woman, becoming engendered by the giantess in this story. The focus may be on the negative consequences of sexual violence, rather than demonising same-sex desires. Although we cannot be certain, it is possible that the lesson being taught here is the negative consequence of rape, and the birthing of children in this context, rather than the negative impact of same sex desires between women. Loki's gender fluidity and pansexuality may therefore appear to be accepted within the context of these myths. Potentially, the myths offer up the idea that fluidity can bring a positive outcome i.e. the birthing of children.

In this context, Loki's acceptance by the Æsir, despite (or because of?) their gender fluidity and dynamic sexuality may attest to the acceptance of gender fluidity and queerness more generally amongst Norse Viking society. In breaking binary constructions of gender and sexuality, Loki gives permission for those in society to do the same. As Lönnroth presents *Völuspá* in relating themes and concepts to a 13th century, relatively Christian, audience, so too do I make the argument that the pre-Christian core of the mythology is receptive to a pre-Christian audience. If we take this basic premise to be true, then we could perhaps accept how this understanding of gender fluidity and its associated queerness may have been given social understanding and acceptance by the Norse of the Viking Age.

This social acceptance will have been modelled by the Æsir, and experienced by Loki. In this religious and sacred context of social acceptance, the Norse may have tolerated—and potentially encouraged—an existence of queer identities as normality. If this is the case, then we may begin to understand a queer acceptance, transformed into something "othered" at the Conversion Period of Christianity.

How this is possible may lie in the introduction of extended written texts, by which transmission of traditional knowledge—in this case social and religious ideas—may have been disjointed from the traditional means of oral transmission. When this happens, the law codes begin to emerge based upon an ecclesiastical perception and enforcement of a moral system. Essentially, Paganism was replaced by Christianity by the time of Snorri Sturluson writing in the 13th century. In this, we can now see what was once hidden, the dynamic religious society of the Norse and their socially relevant experiences.

## Conclusion

The role of Loki in the Norse mythology is a complex one. Comparatively across religions, one can begin to understand the character of Loki to be more than a "trickster," but a defier of order in their role to create balance in chaos. Loki is fiery chaos, fuelled by a desire to fulfil the gods' destiny in Ragnarok.

Loki indeed has a place in the mythology, greater than that of Dumézil's model, and resting upon Frakes' in this attempt to consolidate the nature of Loki—a question pondered by academics across the decades. This thesis has shown that Loki is both a trickster, and an agent of chaos who fulfils the ultimate destiny.

The relationship between Loki and the god Óðinn is an important one, to which Loki finds themselves becoming equal in status to the god, and is counted towards the Æsir despite their subverted birth by a giant man and an Æsir woman. Loki has been shown to subvert both social and sexual norms whereby in a contemporary 13th century setting, their punishment and charges would be brought under the codes of *Grágas*. Yet in the Viking Age, the period prior to full Christianisation, we have found that Loki embodies a queerness of gender and sexuality that may have been accepted within Viking society.

This thesis has outlined that Loki, across the myths, reaches their ultimate destiny through the events of Ragnarok. Loki also queers the events of the myths, in both a pre-Christian context of original stanza texts, but also in the contemporary post-Christian context of the 13th century, owing to acts of sexual perversion under the legal code of *Grágas*.

I hope that Loki will continue to inspire scholarship and the rigours of questioning in terms of their queerness and position within Norse mythology. It is through this consolidation of the Norse worldview that we can begin to fully understand the nature of Loki, and how they relate to the balance of order and chaos in reaching their destiny.

# Translations

# LOKKA TÁTTUR

## translated by Ben Waggoner

*Editor's note:* Lokka Táttur *is a Faroese ballad that likely originated in the late Middle Ages. This valuable piece of folklore reinforces Loki's role in a divine triad with Odin and Hoenir, and tells the tale of Loki saving a human child's life through cleverness, keeping faith with the human farmers who ask for his help. It also provides more intriguing connections between Loki and fish—also seen, for instance, in Snorri's salmon associations with Loki. The current Shope (Publications Director) for the Troth, Ben Waggoner, offers his own English translation here. Readers with a taste for heavy metal might enjoy the somewhat abridged version of this ballad on the 2008 album* Land *by Faroese Viking metal band Týr.*

1. Risin og bondin leikaðu leik,
risin vann og bondin veik.

1. The giant and the farmer played a
   game;
   the giant won and the farmer lost.

*Stev. Hvàt skàl màr harpan undir
mína hond,
vil ikki frægur filgja màr á onnur
lond.*

*Refrain: What can my harp do under
my hands?
Fame won't follow me to other lands.*

2. Eg hàvi lúkað treytir mín',
nú vil eg fáa sonin tín.

2. "I have done what I said I'd do,
now I will take your son.

3. Eg vil hàva sonin frá tàr,
uttan tú goymir hann firi màr.

3. "I will take your son from you,
unless you conceal him from me."

4. Bondin heitir á sveinar tvá:
biðjið Óðin firi meg inngá.

4. The farmer called on two lads:
"Ask Odin to come inside for me.

5. Heitið á Óðin Æsakong,
tá mann goymslan gerast long.

5. "Call on Odin the Æsir-King,
then the hiding will last long.

6. Eg vildi, mín Óðin væri til,
vita hvussu goymslan ganga vil.

6. "I wish my dear Odin were here,
to find out how the hiding will go."

7. Áður enn teir hövdu hálvtàlað
orð,
tá vár Óðin inn firi borð.

7. Before their words were half
spoken,
there was Odin at the table.

8. Hoyr tú Óðin, eg tàli til tín,
tú skalt goyma sonin mín.

8. "Hear me, Odin, I say to you,
you must hide my son."

9. Oðin fór við sveini út,
brúður og bondi bóru sút.

9. Odin went out with the lad;
the wife and husband both were sad.

10. Oðin biður vaxa brátt,
àkurin upp á eini nátt.

10. Odin ordered the field to grow,
grow up quickly, in one night.

11. Óðin biður vera svein
mitt í àkri axið eitt.

11. Odin ordered the boy to be
one ear of grain in the middle of the
field,

12. Mitt í àkri axið eitt,
mitt í axi biggkorn eitt.

12. One ear of grain in the middle of
the field,
one barleycorn on the ear of grain.

13. Ver hàrí við onga pínu,
tá íð eg kalli, kom til mín.

13. "Stay there without pain;
when I call, come to me.

14. Ver hàrí við onga sút,
tá íð eg kalli, kom her út.

14. "Stay there without sorrow;
when I call, come out here."

15. Risin hevir hjarta hart sum
horn,
ripar nú fangið fullt við korn.

15. The giant had a heart as hard as
horn;
he reaped the grain by the armful.

16. Ripar nú korn í fang á sàr,
og bitran brand i hendi bàr.

16. He reaped the grain into his
clutches,
and he bore a sharp sword in his hand.

17. Og bitran brand í hendi bàr,
hann ætlar al högga sveinin hàr.

17. A sharp sword he bore in hand;
he meant to strike the boy there.

18. Tá vàr sveini komin til sút,
biggkorn kreyp úr neva út.

18. When the lad was feeling sorrow,
the barleycorn slipped out of the
giant's fist.

19. Tá vàr sveini komin til pína,
Óðin kallar hann til sín.

19. When the lad was feeling pain,
Odin called him to come.

20. Óðin fór við sveini heim,
bondi og brúður fagna teim.

20. Odin went home with the boy;
the farmer and wife were glad to see
them.

21. Her er hin ungi alvi tín,
nú er uppi goymsla mín.

21. "Here is your young child;
now my guardianship is over."

22. Bondin heitir á sveina tvá:
biðjið Hønir firi meg inngá.

22. The farmer called on two lads:
"Ask Hoenir to come inside for me.

23. Eg vildi, mín Hønir væri til,
vita, hvussu goymslan ganga vil.

23. "I wish my dear Hoenir were
here,
to find out how the hiding will go."

24. Áður enn teir hövdu hálvtàlad
orð,
tá vàr Hønir inn firi borð.

24. Before their words were half
spoken,
there was Hoenir at the table.

25. Hoyr tú Hønir, eg tàli til tín,
tú skalt goyma sonin mín.

25. "Hear me, Hoenir, I say to you,
you must hide my son."

26. Hønir fór við sveini út,
brúður og bondi bóru sút.

26. Hoenir went out with the lad;
the wife and husband both were sad.

27. Hønir gongur á grønari grund,
svànir sjey teir flugu um sund.

27. Hoenir walked to greener ground;
seven swans were flying over the
sound.

28. Firi eystan flugu svànir tveir,
niður hjá Hønir settust teir.

28. Two swans were flying from the
east;
they landed beside Hoenir.

29. Hønir biður nú vera svein
mitt í knokki fjöður ein'.

29. Hoenir ordered the boy to be
one feather in the middle of the head.

30. Ver hàri við onga pínu,
tá íð eg kalli, kom til mín.

30. "Stay there without pain,
when I call, come to me.

31. Ver hàrí við onga sút,
tá íð eg kalli, kom her út.

31. "Stay there without sorrow,
when I call, come out here."

32. Skrýmsli loypur á grønari
grund,
svànir sjey teir flugu um sund.

32. The giant stomped on the greener ground;
seven swans flew over the sound.

33. Risin fell tá á sítt knæ,
tann fremsta svànin fekk hann hàr.

33. The giant fell on one knee,
and there he seized the first swan.

34. Tann fremsta svánin hann àf
beit
hálsin nidur í herðar sleit.

34. He bit the neck of the first swan
and severed it from its body.

35. Tá vàr sveini komin til sút,
fjöður smeyg àf kjafti út.

35. When the lad was feeling sorrow,
the feather squeezed out of the
giant's jaws.

36. Tá var sveini komin til pína,
Hønir kallaði hann til sín.

36. When the lad was feeling pain,
Hoenir called him to come.

37. Hønir fór við sveini heim,
brúður og bondi fagna teim.

37. Hoenir went home with the boy;
the farmer and wife were glad to see
them.

38. Her er hin ungi alvi tín,
nú er uppi goymsla mín.

38. "Here is your young child;
now my guardianship is over."

39. Bondin heitir á sveinar tvá:
biðjið Lokka firi meg inngá.

39. The farmer called on two lads:
"Ask Loki to come inside for me.

40. Eg vildi mín Lokki væri til,
vita, hvussu goymslan ganga vil.

40. "I wish my dear Loki were here,
to find out how the hiding will go."

41. Aður enn teir hövdu hálvtalað
orð,
tá vàr Lokki inn firi borð.

41. Before their words were half
spoken,
there was Loki at the table.

42. Tú veitst einki àf mínari neyð,
Skrýmsli ætlar mín sonar deyð.

42. "You know nothing of my distress:
the monster wants my son dead."

43. Hoyr tú Lokki, eg táli til tín.
tú skalt goyma sonin mín.

43. "Hear me, Loki, I say to you,
you must hide my son.

44. Goym hann væl . so sum tú
kant,
làt ikki Skrýmsli fáa hann.

44. "Hide him well, as best you can:
don't let the ogre catch him!"

45. Skàl eg goyma sonin tín,
tá mást tú lúka treytir mín'.

45. "If I am to hide your son,
you must meet my conditions.

46. Tú skalt làta neystið gera,
meðan eg mann burtur vera.

46. "You must build a boathouse,
while I have to be away.

47. Víðan glugga sker tú á,
jarnkelvi legg tú hár íhjá.

47. "Cut a wide window in it,
put an iron bar high inside it."

48. Lokki fór við sveini út,
brúður og bondi bóru sút.

48. Loki went out with the lad;
the wife and husband both were sad.

49. Lokki gongur eftir sandi,
sum skútan fleyt firí landi.

49. Loki walked along the sand;
a small boat floated by the land.

50. Lokki rør á igsta klakk,
so er í fornum frøði sagt.

50. Loki rowed to the farthest banks,
as is told in the old lore.

| | |
|---|---|
| 51. Lokki hevir ei fleiri orð, | 51. Loki had no more to say; |
| ongul og stein hann varpar firi borð. | he flung a hook and sinker overboard. |

| | |
|---|---|
| 52. Ongul og steinur við grunni vóð, | 52. The hook and sinker soon touched bottom; |
| snarliga higgin hanu flundru dró. | soon he pulled in a flounder. |

| | |
|---|---|
| 53. Dregur hann eina, dregur hann tvá, | 53. He hauled in one, he hauled in two; |
| hin triðja hon vàr svört at sjá. | the third one was black to see. |

| | |
|---|---|
| 54. Lokki biður nú vera svein | 54. Loki ordered the boy to be |
| mitt í rogni kornið eitt. | one egg among the roe. |

| | |
|---|---|
| 55. Ver hàrí við onga pínu, | 55. "Stay there without pain, |
| tá íð eg kalli, kom til mín. | when I call, come to me. |

| | |
|---|---|
| 56. Ver hàrí við onga sút, | 56. "Stay there without sorrow, |
| tá íð eg kalli, kom her út. | when I call, come out here." |

| | |
|---|---|
| 57. Lokki rør nú aftur àt landi, | 57. Now Loki rowed back to land. |
| risin stendur firi honum á sandi. | There stood the giant on the sand. |

| | |
|---|---|
| 58. Risin mælti so orðum brátt: | 58. The giant immediately spoke: |
| Lokki, hvàr hevir tú verið í nátt? | "Loki, where have you been this night?" |

| | |
|---|---|
| 59. Lítla mann eg hàva ró, | 59. "I've had little rest; |
| Flakkað og fàrið um allan sjó. | I've wandered and traveled all over the sea." |

| | |
|---|---|
| 60. Risin oman sin jarnnakka skjýtur, | 60. The giant shoved out his iron boat; |
| Lokki rópar, at ílla brytur. | Loki shouted that the waves were breaking. |

61. Lokki tálar so firi sàr:
risin, làt meg filgja tàr.

61. Loki spoke up and said,
"Giant, let me go with you."

62. Risin tók sàr stýri i hand,
Lokki rør nú út frá land.

62. The giant took the rudder in
hand;
Loki rowed away from land.

63. Lokki rør við langa leið,
ikki vil jarnnakkin ganga úr stáð.

63. Loki rowed for a long time;
the iron boat wouldn't move from its
place.

64. Lokki svör við sína trú;
eg kann betur at stýra enn tú.

64. Loki swore by his faith,
"I can steer better than you."

65. Risin setist til árar at ró,
jarnnakkin fleyg um allan sjó.

65. The giant sat at the oars and rowed;
the iron boat flew all over the sea.

66. Risin rør við langan favn,
næstum Lokka aftur í stavn.

66. The giant rowed with his broad
armspan,
as Loki stood behind him in the prow.

67. Risin rør nú á itsta klakk,
so er í fornum frøði sagt.

67. The giant rowed to the farthest
banks,
as is told in the old lore.

68. Risin hevir ei fleiri orð,
ongul og stein hann varpar firi
borð.

68. The giant had no more to say;
he flung a hook and sinker over-
board.

69. Ongul og steinur við grunni
veður,
snarliga higgin hann flundru dregur.

69. The hook and sinker soon
touched bottom;
soon he pulled in a flounder.

70. Dregur hann eina, dregur hann
tvá,
hin triðja hon vàr svört at sjá.

70. He hauled in one, he hauled in
two;
the third one was black to see.

71. Lokki svör á sína list:
risin, gev màr henda fisk.

71. Loki answered with his cunning,
"Giant, give me that fish."

72. Risin sváraði og segði nei:
nei, mín Lokki, tu fært hann ei.

72. The giant answered, and said no:
"No, dear Loki, you won't get it."

73. Hann setti fisk millum kníja á
sàr,
taldi hvört korn, í rogni var.

73. He set the fish between his
knees;
he counted every egg in the roe.

74. Taldi hvört korn í rogni var,
hann ætlaði fanga sveinin hàr.

74. He counted every egg in the roe;
he meant to catch the boy there.

75. Tá vár sveini komin til sút,
kornið kreyp úr neva út.

75. When the lad was feeling sorrow,
the egg squeezed out of the giant's
fist.

76. Tá vár sveini komin til pína,
Lokki kallar hann til sín.

76. When the lad was feeling pain,
Loki called him to come.

77. Set teg niður firi aftan meg,
lát ikki risan síggja teg.

77. "Sit down and stay behind me,
don't let the giant see you.

78. Tú mást leypa so lattur á land,
ikki merkja spor í sand.

78. "You must dash so lightly on land
that you don't leave tracks on the sand."

79. Risin rør nú aftur til land,
beint ímóti hvítan sand.

79. Now the giant rowed back to land,
straight up to the white sand.

80. Risin rør àt landi tá,
Lokki snýr jarnnakka frá.

80. The giant rowed up to land;
Loki turned the boat around.

81. Risin skjýtur afturstavn á land,
sveinur loypur so lattur á land.

81. The giant shoved the stern onto
land;
the boy dashed so lightly onto land.

82. Risin sàr seg upp á land,
sveinur stendur fíri honum á sand.

83. Sveinur leyp so lattur á land,
ikki merkti spor í sand.

84. Risin leyp so tungur á land
upp til kníja niður í sand.

85. Sveinur leyp sum hann kundi
betst,
leyp í gjögnum faðirs neyst.

86. Hann leyp ígjögnum faðirs
neyst,
risin eftir við fullgott trejst.

87. Risin stóð í glugga fastur,
jarnkelvið í heysi brast.

88. Lokki vàr tá ikki seinur,
hjó àf risanum annað beinið.

89. Risin heldur àt tí gàman,
sárið grøddi snart til sàman.

90. Lokki vàr tá ikki seinur,
hjó àf risanum hit annað beinið.

91. Hjó af honum hit annað bein,
kastaði millum stokk og stein.

82. The giant looked up to the land—
the boy stood before him on the sand.

83. The boy dashed so lightly onto
land,
he left no tracks on the sand.

84. The giant charged so heavily
onto land,
he sank to his knees in the sand.

85. The boy dashed as best he could;
he dashed right through his father's
boathouse.

86. He dashed right through his
father's boathouse;
the giant followed, quite confident.

87. The giant got stuck fast in the
window—
the iron bar struck him on the head.

88. Loki didn't waste any time:
he cut off one of the giant's legs.

89. The giant was rather amused:
the wound quickly grew together.

90. Loki didn't waste any time:
he cut off the giant's other leg.

91. He cut off his other leg,
and threw a log and a stone in between.

92. Sveinur higgur á við gáman
hvussu risin leyp bæði sundir og
  sáman.

92. The boy observed with amusement
how the giant ran, cut apart and
  together.

93. Lokki fór við sveini heim,
brúður og bondi fagna teim,

93. Loki went home with the boy;
the farmer and wife were glad to
  see them.

94. Her er hin ungi alvi tín,
nú er uppi goymslan mín.

94. "Here is your young child;
now my guardianship is over.

95. Nú er uppi goymslan mín,
eg hàvi lúkað treytir tínar.

95. "Now my guardianship is over;
I have done what you asked me to
  do.

96. Eg hàvi hildið trú firi visst,
nú hevir risin lívið misst.

96. "I have surely kept faith;
now the giant has lost his life."

Original text: Hammershaimb, V. U. *Sjúrðar Kvæði: Udgivne af det Nor-
diske Literatur-Samfund*. København: Bröderne Berlings Bogtryk-
keri, 1851.

*Drawing of Loki from the "Melsteðs-Edda" Icelandic manuscript,
copied and illustrated by Jakob Sigurðsson, 1765-6.
Stofnun Árna Magnússonar, SÁM 66. Courtesy of Handrit.is. Public Domain.*

# Recipes

## LOKI INCENSE

**by Törik Björnulf**

### Ingredients

**Wood base:**
Powdered red sandalwood

*This was chosen as the base for the blend, but also for its red color. I often associated the color red with Loki.*

**Herbs/spices:**
Tobacco
Allspice
Rosemary

*The herbs in this recipe I was drawn to based on intuition, rather than choosing them. I just had a feeling that these herbs and spices could be associated with Loki.*

**Resin:**
Frankincense

*Frankincense is often associated with the element of fire, and Loki is also often associated with fire.*

**Oils:**
Vanilla
Lavender

*The oils chosen for this blend were for their soft notes and their association with feminine energies. Loki being a Jötunn shapeshifter is able to change not only shape and form, but gender as well. The soft notes of the oils, mixed with the strong notes of the allspice and frankincense, perfectly blend the gender fluidity that represents Loki.*

**Directions**

In a mortar and pestle, grind the herbs, spices, and resin, until desired consistency.

Mix in the powdered red sandalwood. (It is important to use a spoon for this process to minimize the mess—though this is for Loki, so a mess could be expected and appreciated.)

Finally add in 6-8 drops of each oil and stir that into your mix.

While I'm making this blend, I perform galdr by chanting Loki's name. Example: "*Lowwwwwwww-keeeeeeeeeeee*"

I like to add my breath to the mix in between chants. You can also speak an invocation to Loki if you wish.

Example:

*Hail to Loki! Serpent Father! World Creator and World Breaker! Bringer of Truth and Chaos! Bring me laughter, light my inner fire, allow me to seek truth and pursue what I desire! Hail to you! Loki! Lóðurr! Sætere! HAIL!*

*"Three-god bracteate" from Gudme II, Fyn, Denmark.*
*In the most common interpretation, the figure at the left is thought to be Loki,*
*the central figure is Balder, and the rightmost figure, holding a spear, is Odin.*
*Photo by Lennart Larsen, National Museum of Denmark. CC BY-SA 4.0.*

# Contributors

## FLY AMANITA

Fly Amanita is a lifelong weirdo and disciple of defamiliarization who prefers to spend time in the garden or the woods. If one must be inside, she thinks it best to be in possession of a pencil or some crayons, a guitar, some sort of drum, or a piano.

## LUKE BABB

Luke Babb (they/them) is a devotional polytheist, a skeptical spirit worker, and a magical Jack of all Trades. Their work focuses on the gods of Iceland and Greece, as well as the queer spirits of the Fellowship of the Phoenix. More of their creative nonfiction can be found in their monthly column at *The Wild Hunt*.

## TÖRIK BJÖRNULF

Törik Björnulf is a practitioner of inclusive heathenry, crafter, author, and ally to the LGBTQ community. Although not always an active member of the heathen community, he contributes to his fellow heathen friends by being a seeker of knowledge and providing that knowledge to both new and experienced practitioners to use at their leisure. Having experience in multiple subjects such as devotional work, runic magic, and fjölkingy, he offers his work and studies in not only his writings and recipes, but also his crafts.

## BAT COLLAZO

Bat Collazo is a queer Heathen of color, writer, editor, crafter, and visual artist. Bat's spiritual path focuses on zir oath to Loki, and the worship of gods from each of the three Norse pantheons. Ze also maintains an eclectic practice with a few other deities, and honors spirits of the land, zir ancestors of blood from Poland and Borikén (Puerto Rico), and zir ancestors of choice. Bat community builds towards social change, urban homesteads, and, occasionally, does some ill-advised, untrained Wagnerian opera singing. Ze hopes to complete clergy training through the Troth. Find zir at **batcollazo.com** or on Instagram **@batcollazo**.

## INDIA HOGAN

India writes rituals with the central idea that prayer is protest, and protest is prayer. By identifying and emphasizing the features of ritual that serve the goals of education, peer support and community building, religious observances become opportunities for positive social change.

## JENNJENN

JennJenn has been a follower of Loki for about seven years now.

## KATRINA KUNSTMANN

Katrina Kunstmann is a Lokean Heathen freelance illustrator, writer, comic creator currently based in California. Despite earnest pleadings from the Mother of Monsters, she looked elsewhere until at a Loki focused pagan meet-up local to her county, she had an exceptionally electric epiphany, and has been enamored ever since. She is currently working on three self published comics, one of which concerns Loki himself titled "Mother of Monsters", and the design featured in her illustration is the one that rings most true to her.

## MELANIE LOKADOTTIR

Melanie Lokadottir (she/they) has been a Heathen since 2012 and a member of the Troth since 2018. She practices seidr and does spirit-work and moundsitting. Melanie is oathed to Loki, Sigyn, and Angrboda, and is fulltrui to Their families. She also works on and off with Freya, Thor, Frigg, Veles (of the Slavic pantheon), Perun (of the Slavic pantheon), and a variety of landwights and other spirits. Melanie is also a godspouse to both Freyr and Morana (of the Slavic pantheon). She is currently working on a series of trials for Loki, Angrboda, Sigyn, and Hel. Her goal is to someday complete the Troth's clergy program.

## SAE LOKASON

Sae Lokason is a visual artist, educator, author, and podcaster. He is currently on the High Rede and have been admitted to the clergy program. He has been active within the Lokean community for close to ten years, and a member of the Troth since 2016. He lives in Colorado, and his work can be found at HHH, in Idunna, and at saelokason.com.

## AMY MARSH

Amy Marsh, Ed.D. is a clinical sexologist, certified hypnotist, writer, activist, and solitary practitioner of eclectic witchery. Ze is oathed to Loki Laufeyjarson and also works with Freyr, Gerda, and Freya. Ze currently lives with seven cats in sight of volcanic Mt. Konocti in Lake County, CA. Ze is the mother of two young adults. Ze has endured the social isolation of environmental illness/multiple chemical sensitivity for thirty years. Find zir personal writing at ladyofthelake.blog and guild-of-ornamental-hermits.com.

## OLIVER LEON PORTER

Oliver Leon Porter is a queer trans man who has been called to sip from Óðrœrir, the Mead of Poetry. Oliver is an award-winning teacher and journalist. His poetry has been published in *Eternal Haunted Summer*, an online pagan magazine under the name "Oliver Leôn Hêrês." He lives on unceded Kanien'Keha;ka (Mohawk) territory as a white-skinned settler in Canada. He often teaches tarot to his students once they finish their exams. When not teaching or writing, he can be found cross-stitching. You can find his complete list of works here: https://oliverlporter.wordpress.com/

## LAR MELBYE ROMSDAL

Lar is a practicing Heathen, an international librarian and archivist, and vegetarian. This paper represents their devotion to the Gods and in particular, to the God Loki who is a special person in their life. Lar likes to read, study, and gain knowledge on a range of issues, experiences, and knowledges (as the All-Father intended). Their interests include writing poetry, reading, learning, languages, and exploring.

## PHYLLIS STEINHAUSER

Phyllis began to call herself pagan in 1991, about the same time she enlisted in the Illinois National Guard and went off to college. She soon found some others of a like mind and quickly became ubiquitous in Chicago-area Neopagan events and ritual groups, learning how to organize and facilitate group rituals. Despite many years of exploring, she still hadn't quite found her spiritual niche, but fortunately, in 2005, she joined the Troth, and decided she was Heathen. Ultimately she became the steward for Illinois and served till 2010, when she became the High Steward for The Troth, serving till 2013. During her service, she founded the weekly (Tuesday) Online Heathen Chat (2006), organized IlliniMoot, an annual spring campout, and became the leader of Linden Oak Kindred (2007-2014) while also managing to complete her undergrad degree and earn a Paralegal certificate. During that time, she also gave many talks and presentations about Heathen/Asatru ritual/practice at Pagan festivals, Pagan Pride Days, and by invitation to various local groups upon request. After relocating to The Left Coast in 2016, she has again become active in the community as a founding member of Cascadia Freehold in Portland, Oregon.

## DYRI VIXEN

Dyri Vixen is a parent and Lokean artist whose work focuses on the family ties Loki values as a deity with several children. Both as a mother and as a father, Loki is a deity whose nature is seen in the footsteps of a child dancing to a rhythmless song without words, in the the flagrant disregard for societal expectations of the youth seeking their own voice, and in the inner child reconciling all fears and hopes accumulating over a lifetime of adults who continue the cycles of life. Parenthood is itself chaotic, and for all parents whose focus lies within The Troth, Loki can be a very loving guide in helping us to remain aware of the child as a growing fire of its own, no longer just the spark from our own flames.

## BEN WAGGONER

Ben Waggoner is the author of 12 translations from Old Norse and Old English, and currently serves the Troth as its Publications Director. He has been studying Old Norse for over 15 years. He is a founding member of Black Bear Kindred of Central Arkansas, married to his gorgeous wife Mandy, and has a lively son who is a born Thorsman. Ben also co-hosts the Heathen History Podcast with Lauren Crow. In his copious spare time, he is a college professor.

## ELEANOR WOOD

Eleanor is based in the UK and is sometimes found at the Hendon Heathens moot.

**Illustration Sources:**

Bray, Olive; W. G. Collingwood, illus. *The Elder or Poetic Edda, Commonly Known as Sæmund's Edda. Vol. 1: The Mythological Poems.* London: The Viking Club, 1908.

Brown, Abbie Farwell; E. Boyd Smith, illus. *In the Days of Giants: A Book of Norse Tales.* Boston: Houghton Mifflin, 1902.

Calverley, William Slater; W. G. Collingwood, ed. *Notes on the Early Sculptured Crosses, Shrines and Monuments in the Present Diocese of Carlisle.* Kendal: T. Wilson, 1899.

Guerber, Hélène. *Myths of the Norsemen from the Eddas and Sagas.* London: George G. Harrap, 1919.

The Troth is an international organization that brings together many paths and traditions within Germanic Heathenry, such as Ásatrú, Theodish Belief, Urglaawe, Forn Sed, and Anglo-Saxon Heathenry. We welcome all who have been called to follow the elder ways of Heathenry, and who have heard the voices of the Gods and Goddesses of Heathenry, our ancestors, the landvættir, and the spirits around us.

The Troth is an inclusive Heathen organization. We welcome all who feel drawn to honor the old gods, regardless of race, ethnicity, or gender identification.

To find out more about our organization or to join us, visit **http://www.thetroth.org/**, contact us at **troth-questions@thetroth.org**, or look for us on Facebook at **https://www.facebook.com/groups/TheTroth/**

Our complete line of books and back issues of our journal *Idunna* may be viewed at **https://www.lulu.com/spotlight/thetroth**

For book reviews, interviews, or any other matters connected with our publications, please contact us at **troth-shope@thetroth.org**

Ingram Content Group UK Ltd.
Milton Keynes UK
UKHW022203220323
419017UK00015B/177/J